# In the Shelter
# of the Oak

## Finding Positive Direction
## on a Tragic Life Path

**By Barbara Rowe Colvin, MSCP**

D1468516

# In the Shelter of the Oak

Although this is a work of nonfiction, a number of names have been changed as a courtesy in keeping with the author's standards of modesty, propriety and decorum.

Printed in the United States of America

ISBN # 1505204119

ISBN: 13 # 9781505204117

Library of Congress Control Number: 2014921321

CreateSpace Independent Publishing Platform

North Charleston, South Carolina

Portions of the article, *Voices of Anger,* reprinted with permission of the author

Edited by Lynn White

Cover design by Jack Daily

*This book is dedicated to:*

*My parents, grandparents, aunts and uncles, my brother, my late husband Charles,*
*My children,*
*Victims of crime and parents who have outlived their children,*
*Teenagers who are sure they have all the answers,*
*And to my husband Ed who has allowed me to close my past and look forward to my*
*future*

# In the Shelter of the Oak

*Barbara Colvin*

*Matthew 17:20*

# *Introduction*
### *By Ed Colvin*

It was March of 1958 when I first met Barbara. I was wandering the first floor halls of Phillips High School in Birmingham, Alabama. Barbara, a hall marshal, was sitting at her station in the front hall. I rounded the corner. It was class time, and I was not supposed to be in the halls without a legitimate reason, which I did not have. She was a pretty girl, and I struck up a conversation about why she shouldn't report me...she didn't.

We double-dated one or two times that spring, but she was fourteen and I was fifteen, neither of us drove and we lived too far apart, so we took separate paths. How could we know that we would eventually find one another again years later?

When we reconnected almost fifty years later, we had each had a share of grief. Her resilience is amazing. What does it take to get up off the ground when you have been knocked down again and again? It takes the qualities of a champion, determination and inner strength, not to give up. Barbara Colvin is a champion in my eyes. When we first met, back in high school, she was living with her brother because her father, mother and grandparents had all died. At fifteen, I could not begin to fathom the grief and pain she had already suffered. She had been knocked down hard by age fourteen, yet she was facing life with determination and a beautiful smile. Forty years later, preparing for a high school reunion, I read the bio she had written for the reunion book where she listed her husband and children as deceased. Again, I could not imagine that sort of grief and pain as I had not experienced anything like it.

Several years later, I found myself knocked down by grief after the loss of my wife. I was in a deep valley and not sure I could get up. I found Barbara, and we talked about life and death and how she persevered to get up off the ground and not give up on living. Her example helped pull me out of the valley and stand up again.

Barbara has revealed her amazing story in this memoir and hopes her story can help others turn their own grief into a positive direction of fulfillment and affirmation of life.

I am so lucky to have found her again.

# *My Mission*

To inspire the broken-hearted to do all they can to help themselves, and to leave the rest to God.

"THE PRESENT IS THE LIVING SUM-TOTAL OF THE PAST"
THOMAS CARLYLE

## Chapter One

How do you find the strength to keep standing when tragedies explode around you as if you walked through a field of land mines? One minute can be spent out in the open and seeing a way forward when, with the next step, comes KABOOM! Whatever hope of moving forward in that direction just explodes.

I was loved and wanted; I never doubted that. Many times my adoptive parents shared the story of the trip to Montgomery when they chose me of the three babies up for adoption that day in the fall of 1943. I had been born with asthma, and Mother said I looked like I needed more love and help than the other two. It was my lucky day for sure.

The day my parents were on their way to the orphanage, Daddy was so excited he was stopped by a police officer for speeding. Mother was bursting at the seams to tell the officer they were traveling to Montgomery to pick up their new baby girl. The officer let them go with a warning saying, "If I'm on duty when you come back, I want to see her."

Who is the baby girl born as Nancy Faye Norwood, renamed Barbara Benton? And who will she become? I was born to an unwed mother in the Bible Belt of the south in April of 1943 and adopted, at six months of age, by extraordinary parents. I am no stranger to tragedy, and no one can call me a coward. I have spent years trying to pick up the pieces of a shattered life and refusing to let tragedy define me. My faith has allowed me to turn personal adversity into triumph and given me an avenue to help others. I am proud to have taken on opportunities presented to me to make a difference in the lives of those suffering from grief and loss. I am a survivor.

Mine was an idyllic early childhood. My family lived in an old, rambling house in the North Highlands neighborhood in Birmingham, Alabama. My brother, Freddy, my parents' biological child, was five years older. Daddy's parents lived in the house also. I was the only girl in a family of boys—my brother Freddy and my two cousins, Frankie, who was close to my age and Billy, several years older. I had confidence and clout and an attitude to match.

I was never sure if my grandparents owned the house and we lived with them, or if my dad owned the house and his parents lived with us. They were just always there. Having my grandparents around was a marvelous thing for a little girl. My busy, hard-working parents were able to spend only a few precious hours with us each day, but I had plenty of love and attention from Grandma and Cap, my granddaddy. I wasn't sure why we called him Cap, but we did. Grandmother rocked me in front of the fireplace where I felt the warmth of her love. She fixed my scraped knees and dried my tears when life was too rough for my tender years. My grandparents took me to movies and treated me to ice cream delights at Grayson's Spinning Wheel Ice Cream Parlor that looked like a fake igloo with a polar bear on the roof. Cap hoisted me on his shoulders at the annual Veterans parade so I could see above the crowd. Dark clouds on the horizon could not have been farther from my young mind.

For the day-to-day needs of a small child, our nanny, Mary Britton, who raised my father and my brother, was now raising me. She was a lady who cared for me and loved me like her own and I surely loved her back. We shared a bedroom with twin beds until the day my mother died. Mary took care of me in the night when my asthma troubled me, holding me up so I could breathe more easily. I once sneaked my brother's baseball glove out of the house to play ball in the park and hurt my back sliding into home base. Mary was alarmed at the injury and comforted me by rubbing my back with healing salve as she shook her hands over me to 'shake the evil spirits out.'

Daddy always said Mary took care of us growing up and we would take care of her all her life. His loving attitude toward her gave me a sense of caring and responsibility. We were also blessed with a devoted housekeeper, Leslie Shepherd. Mother and Daddy worked side by side in the family business, so these two ladies were home to mother me during the day and showed me even more love than my own family. Eventually, it fell to my brother to take care of Mary until she died after passing her 100th birthday.

The family business was Benton Brothers Dyers and Dry Cleaners, with a main cleaning plant and four dry cleaning branch offices. Most dry cleaners have their plant on the premises now, but then the cleaning was done at a central location. There was also a cold storage vault where the bigger department stores and furriers in downtown Birmingham stored furs. The business was busy and successful and provided a comfortable living for our family. I learned valuable lessons about how hard work provides that comfortable lifestyle. Life was good.

In 1951, when I was eight years old, my grandmother, Margaret Kernahan Benton, became ill and spent a lot of time in bed with a lingering illness, possibly cancer, but I didn't even know what that was back then. She passed away that year. I remember feeling disappointed and a little mad because she had promised to take me to the movies when she was feeling better. Not quite understanding what was going on, I was included in all the plans and arrangements that had to be made and I observed the reactions of those around me. That was the beginning of my understanding of death and the life to come in heaven.

I adored my big brother, but we were never really close. Five years is a big age gap for siblings, and Freddy didn't think much of my efforts to show how much I admired him. If I snuck in and borrowed one of his shirts to wear, he would never wear it again. As a little girl, I would sleepwalk, go into his room and take all of the treasures from his display shelf to bring into my room. Freddy didn't appreciate my wanderings, but Mother told me she watched my night prowlings with delight.

After school and on Saturdays, my brother and I went to the plant to help out. My duties were to sort the receipts and, with Mother's help, to wait on customers. In those days, customers were *always* right. With good southern upbringing and apprentice training, I learned to say, "Yes, ma'am," "Yes, sir" and "Thank you." Sometimes Mother allowed me to fold the freshly ironed shirts and help with the mending. I think this was our parents' way of teaching us what making a living was all about. As children, there was also a considerable amount of fun as Freddy and I pushed one another through the plant in the laundry carts. Sometimes he would lock me in the cold storage vault and turn the lights off. Mother always came quickly to my rescue, and Freddy got a scolding for that! Still, life was good.

My father was an excellent salesman. He took a lot of Dale Carnegie courses and was President of the City Salesmen's Club. There was a lot of reading material about the power of positive thinking in our house, as well as Christian books, including the works of Peter and Catherine Marshall and Norman Vincent Peale. I also had the strong influence of my Aunt Lillian having to care for Uncle Walter and her frequent advice: "Get your education."

My Aunt Lillian, Daddy's sister, and Uncle Walter lived nearby. Aunt Lillian was my rock, the Christian staple in my life. I loved to visit her church, Third Presbyterian in Birmingham. Her minister, Brother Jimmy, always sang *Heavenly Sunshine* as I walked up the aisle to sit with my aunt as she came out of the choir. His recognition made me feel very special. From Aunt Lillian I learned strength of character. She served as superintendent of the church's Sunday School Department for over thirty years. Through her I learned about trusting in God, being loyal, always trying to do the right thing and being kind to others. Uncle Walter had been seriously injured in World War II, received a Purple Heart medal, and when he came home, was unable to ever work again. Every night before turning out the lights, they read a chapter of the Bible to each other. They read through the Bible many times throughout the years. As the household breadwinner, Aunt Lillian worked for the County Board of Education for thirty-five years. She was promoted as far as she could be with her limited high school education. Often she advised me to get a college degree so I would be able to take care of myself if I ever had to.

I was a quiet child with olive skin, a mop of curly dark hair and large dark eyes in a tiny face. As a little girl, I played tea party with my neighborhood playmates. We dressed up in grown-up outfits, served tea in little tea cups and talked about flowers, our hair and all manner of what we perceived as lady-like conversations. I talked about how smart my pretend children were and how I baked cookies for my grandchildren and took them to the movies.

There was never any mystery or secret about my being adopted. From an early age, Mother read a little book about it to me—even before I could understand what adoption meant. She always told me if I wanted to find my biological mom, she would be glad to help me. As many adopted children can attest, some of us have an intense curiosity about our biological families and who they might be or just want to gather medical information. Others have little or no interest in their biological origins.

We lived in an area where there were a lot of Italian families. As I sat in my classroom, I looked at other children who looked like me. I convinced myself that I must have come from an Italian family and decided I'd better start going to the Catholic Church because that's where my Italian schoolmates went to church. Although we attended the Presbyterian Church, I told Mother I wanted to take Catechism classes to become a Catholic. Mother always let me be whoever I wanted to be, so I took some instruction from the local priest. I never did become a Catholic, but was grateful for the freedom to try to find my past in this way. I wanted to find my own identity.

Our family life was geared toward business. The love was always present, but there was not a lot of laughter and hugging in our household. We didn't take vacations and travel much, but my parents owned a Fish Camp on Lake Talquin in north Florida, between Quincy and Tallahassee. It had a number of cabins and a main dining room and was patronized mostly by doctors, lawyers and businessmen who wanted to rent a cabin for a few days to spend time fishing. We went there several times a year for a short stay, in our private rooms above the mess hall, to check up on the camp management and for a bit of relaxation for my parents. There was a huge bell down by the lake that the cooks rang when breakfast, lunch or dinner was served. Freddy and I always raced to the lake's edge hoping to be the first to ring the bell. One of our cooks, Matilda, would often whisper in my ear, "Go pull the bell," so I could get a head start.

One day, Freddy, Daddy, our cocker spaniel, Tinker, and I were out fishing in a small boat. Tinker got a fish hook in his paw and tried to get it out with his teeth. When the hook became lodged in his mouth, Tinker started yelping, I started screaming, and the boat began rocking; it almost turned upside down. Poor Daddy was working to cut the hook out of the dog's mouth while trying to keep me calm at the same time. It was probably not the best day of fishing for Freddy and Daddy, to say the least.

In addition to time at the fish camp, Freddy and I spent a week every summer with our Aunt Allie on her farm in Soddy Daisy, Tennessee. Possum Creek ran near her property, and we had great experiences swimming in the creek, as well as collecting eggs from the chicken coop and milking the neighbor's cow, Bessie. Bessie made me feel just a little bit superior to my big brother because she didn't like boys and chased Freddy around the pasture and over the fence.

I was twelve years old in 1955 when my daddy, Frederick Karl Benton, Sr., died suddenly from an aneurysm in his heart. Mother had taken me roller skating at our local rink, and she received a phone call that Daddy was sick; she should come home right away. We sped through the streets with Mother flashing the headlights and waving a white handkerchief out the window. Daddy had been on his way up the stairs in our house and called down to my grandfather for help. By the time we arrived he had already passed of a major heart attack. We cried, but Mother expected me to be brave and assured me Daddy was happy and well in heaven. Observing her strength was part of what kept *me* going through all the heartaches yet to come. There was nothing we could do for Daddy, so I was sent to class the next day. Brokenhearted, I came home after only half a day—the only school I missed in eight years of grammar school.

The very next year, 1956, my grandfather Cap, Hugh Karl Benton, died of a heart attack while waiting at a trolley stop. Another brush with courage and loss, another funeral to plan. During the funeral and visitation, Brother Jimmy from the Third Presbyterian Church and many friends came over to pay their respects. I was included in every plan—never shielded—while Mother kept her arms around me. We pictured them all in heaven together. I felt sad, but strong. Mother had a competent business mind and went on to successfully run the business. She was a strong and courageous woman. Life was still good.

After graduating from Martin Grammar School, I started at Phillips High School in September of 1957. Phillips' hardwood floors, shiny and polished, smelled of floor wax and seemed to stretch forever through the miles of painted corridors. I served as one of the dutiful hall monitors. We had a school spirit proclaiming, "We are the best!" and we knew it. We had superb teachers who drilled the importance of learning and the fear of God into teenage heads. This downtown school stood firmly on its reputation as 'Queen of the Big 5.'

Phillips was highly rated in state football in the 1950s. After the games, we went to Ed Salem's, a neighborhood drive-in famous for its curbside service, burgers, barbeque and lemon ice-box pie. This was our hangout and everyone from the area was there. We parked and caught up on all the gossip. If someone got a traffic ticket, he or she would go from car to car collecting change to pay the ticket. There were heated games at the pinball machine where everyone tried to get the highest score. I dated some of the boys my age, but they didn't seem mature enough for my plan of growing up quickly, graduating early and moving ahead with my life.

My secure situation was not to continue. After my father's death, my mother, Mildred Ragland Benton, remarried. On October 13, 1957 as my mother and her new husband were out for supper, she was suddenly stricken with a heart attack and passed away in moments. I felt stunned and broken that night. At the age of fourteen, my life was crumbling as the strong adults in my life had all disappeared, one by one.

A classmate came over to my house to offer some comfort after my mother's passing. Although he never knew it, what he said to me then was a turning point in my grieving process. He spoke from his heart and said, "Barbara, your parents are walking on streets of gold. They're in heaven with Jesus, but what in the world are *you going to do?*"

At that moment it was as though somebody lifted a heavy burden off of me. I felt infallible. The image of those streets of gold lifted my heart, and I was no longer worried about me. I knew I would be okay. After all, I was fourteen, and I knew *all* the answers—or so I thought. That night God threw a blanket of love over me, and He has carried me ever since. The answers would come. I would finish school, get married, have babies and my life would be normal again.

*50 Years later the Phillips High School floors shine on for others.*

*Benton Brother Dyers and Cleaners*

*Much Loved Little Girl*                *Barbara talks to Santa*

"EXPERIENCE: THAT MOST BRUTAL OF TEACHERS.
BUT YOU LEARN, MY GOD DO YOU LEARN."
C. S. LEWIS

# *Chapter Two*

My brother Freddy was a young, married man of nineteen when I went to live with him and his wife Wanda. They had a beautiful home in Vestavia Hills, where living "over the mountain" was *the* place to be. My brother and I had a good start on life thanks to the forward-thinking planning of our parents. It must not have been easy for this young couple to take in a teenager, but I was wrapped up in my own life plan. The only thing I wanted to do at that time was to get married, have a house of my own and a family of my own. In my mind, that was the only way I could feel a sense of belonging again. That fixation was my main worry—when I should have been enjoying my high school years and out having fun. Determined to graduate early, I earned credits through four seasons of summer school and graduated in three years instead of four, missing out on some of the best times in life—my teenage years.

I felt alone and empty inside. Something was missing. Shades Mountain Baptist Church stood near my brother's house, so I decided to attend, meet new friends and become involved. By the end of that year, I decided to join the church and asked God to settle the unrest in my life. My sixteenth birthday was on Easter Sunday in April, 1959. I was baptized that day, and in my prayers I begged for a mentor or an angel to appear and point me in the right direction.

The day after Easter, I tested for my driver's license. Even though I didn't have a car, the license gave me a tremendous sense of freedom. During my sophomore year I participated in an occupation program where students went to school half days and worked half days. I had been saving my paychecks from my after school office job at Steel City Oldsmobile and planned to buy my own car as soon as I could gather enough money.

One weekend evening, I was at a high school girlfriend's house when her older sister asked me, "Would you want to go on a blind date? The guy I'm dating has somebody who would like to meet you." I accepted.

The blind date turned out to be my future husband, Charles Rowe, age twenty-four, who lived on his own, wore business suits and wing-tip shoes, had a job and drove an enviable MGA sports car—all very impressive. A few months later we were married.

I lied to my brother and told him I was spending the night with a friend the weekend Charles and I ran off to Cedartown, Georgia for our secret wedding. We checked in at the courthouse, but came out dejected after being told we couldn't get married without parental consent because I was underage. An old man sitting on the courthouse steps told us we could go to a nearby church where the preacher would marry us. We were married by that preacher March 5, 1960. After I graduated from high school in the summer of 1960, Charles told my brother we were husband and wife, and we moved into an apartment in Homewood. Everyone predicted our marriage wouldn't last, but my defiant teenage personality made me all the more determined to make this marriage work.

How "wise" I was at sixteen. I *knew* what was best for me and that was what I was going to do. I had *all* the answers. I was too smart to take

Charles home to meet my brother and guardian. Charles had convinced me to keep our wedding a secret for a few months before telling Freddy, to give me time to finish high school so that my brother wouldn't have our marriage annulled. Though I *thought* I was smart about my life, I made some ill-advised decisions.

Mother had left me with a comfortable trust fund which included a financial provision for my education, but Charles told me he would take care of me and that I didn't need to go to college. His lack of a college degree had never hurt him, he declared. His mantra was, "No wife of mine will ever work." I took the college entrance exam anyway, but failed the math portion. Just after taking a remedial math course so I could pass the exam, I became pregnant. Our first son, Charles E. Rowe, Jr.—whom we called Chuck, was born after we'd been married only a year and a half.

Chuck's birth was a marvel to me. As an adopted child, I felt for the first time what a miracle it is to pass along part of myself as well as part of my husband to a new little person. Not only was this infant part of the Rowe heritage, but also part of my birth parents. Charles's mother, whom we called Granny, pleased me so much when she told me I was an excellent mother. I believe I worked very hard to be a good, responsible parent and to be loved by my children and my husband.

From the start, Charles and I had different ideas about how family life should be. He expected me to stay in my "place"—at home with our boys, where he was the head of the household and I was supposed to please him above all. This caused me great anguish as my conflicting feelings told me marriage should be a partnership. Charles was a product of his generation, and many of those beliefs we find so out-of-touch today were fairly normal views at the time. While Charles was a good provider and loved his family very much, he believed women were to care for the household and the man should take care of all the decisions regarding the family's future. To me, he filled the place of father, mother, lover and friend. But because

I was so young, I still wanted to find out just who I was and where I was going as a person. Many times I experienced the flight or fight response, but I adapted to each situation and, as time passed, I became convinced that God would reward me in time. Looking back, I am now grateful for those years at home with my children.

Charles had grown up in a household where his parents fought a lot. He made it clear that we would not do the same. If we couldn't get along, he reasoned, we would divorce. He would be the man of the house and make the decisions or things would not work out for us. I agreed.

Charles had three sisters and a brother and all of us met at his parents' house most weekends and holidays. I was glad to have his mother's help to teach me to cook and sew and she bragged about how smart I had become since joining their family.

Six weeks after Chuck our first baby was born, we moved from an apartment into our new home. We had purchased three and a half acres in Indian Springs just south of the Vestavia Hills area of greater Birmingham. We built a home next to Double Oak Mountain State Park. Charles put a salt block in front of our home and wild deer would come into the yard. I kept a clean house, washed and ironed all of Charles' shirts and washable trousers and did my share of the yard work.

Aunt Lillian's advice about education still rang true for me. After taking that remedial math course, I tried the exam once more and passed, but before I could enroll in college classes, I became pregnant with our second son Jeff, so my college plans were frustrated once again. Our son, Jeffrey Benton Rowe, was born June 11, 1964, and I settled into my role as mother. Charles was pleased to be the father of two sons to carry on the Rowe name, the only boys in his family.

Charles was working for Hayes Aircraft, a government contractor that updated and maintained military aircraft. A few years later, the company went through a restructuring and Charles was laid off. He decided he didn't ever want to work for another person again, but wanted to be in an enterprise of his own.

He was offered a business opportunity that interested him and partnered with a seasoned contractor to form a new construction company where the partner designed and drew blueprints and Charles built the new homes.

Charles built a four-stall stable near the back of our property and we bought two horses—Blue, a Tennessee Walker and Brigitte, a quarter horse, as well as a pony for the boys. We rode through the adjacent state park and marveled at the awesome beauty of God's creation. Charles and I joined a duplicate bridge club, and we bought a boat so the boys could learn to water ski. Jeff named the 22-foot cabin cruiser the "Rowe Boat." Life was good.

A downturn in the economy in the late 60s caused financial difficulties for our business as well as most businesses in the United States. During this period my father-in-law passed away, and Charles lost an eye in a firecracker accident. We sold our house to pay Charles' business debts and moved "temporarily" to an apartment, supposedly for about six months. That six months turned into a four and a half year stay. I remember those years as being lonely, confusing and hurtful. The boys and I joined the nearby Presbyterian church. Though he loved to listen to gospel music, Charles had had a bad experience at church in his childhood and refused to attend services with us.

I learned to buy groceries in quantity during the 60s because we lived far out of town and we could save money and time by not going to the store too often. I bought bushels of fresh vegetables at the curb market and prepared them for the freezer. My life revolved around our children and our home. I had requested that the boys attend Christian school, and they did from the first grade on. I obtained my real estate license and was using my income from real estate sales to pay the private school tuition.

The flexibility of the real estate job allowed me to be home when my boys came home from school. I volunteered with the PTA and as room mother.

Charles had his work, his hobbies, the yard work and his buddies. I was not to worry about anything because he would take care of things. I was only to be concerned about the housework and getting supper on the table. He considered any work around the house as "woman's work" and did not offer to help. His reasoning—he worked and all I ever did was stay home. Not exactly my viewpoint, but that was his unwavering belief.

It was difficult for me to watch Charles struggle over what business would make him happy. He finally designed a car wash and service station and built it on the commercial downtown property that had been part of my inheritance, as well as purchasing an adjoining lot to accommodate the building. Civic Center Citgo & Car Wash opened around 1970. I was there most days from 9 a.m. until 2, or until the boys came home from school. My job was to work the cash register, type the bills to be mailed and occasionally make a bank deposit.

Charles had a reciprocal deal with a woman from the local radio station. She gave him free advertising for the business in exchange for free gasoline and car maintenance. This woman was everything Charles always referred to as "cheap and disgusting." Yet his demeanor and language indicated quite a different perspective. I let him know how I felt, but she seemed to chase him all the more. I became jealous enough that he asked her not to come around when I was there. That was not a solution as far as I was concerned. He was working seven days a week, opening at 7 a.m. and closing at 8 p.m., but it was often 11 p.m. before he would get home. I was losing weight worrying about a possible affair between them and considered getting a divorce. I couldn't prove any of my suspicions, however, and the business was sold a few years later. I believe all marriages have their low spots, and this was one of ours.

Charles's cousin asked if he'd be interested in developing eighty acres of property near a country club northwest of Birmingham. This would be a four-way partnership, with Charles eventually owning fifty-one percent of the venture. He sold me on the idea with the stipulation that he wouldn't take out a mortgage on our personal home to do it. I never wanted to lose my home again due to economic downturns. Charles ended up being the most active partner, building about a dozen homes on the best of the acreage, doing the landscaping and keeping the subdivision looking attractive. He developed the infrastructure, putting in roads and water and sewer lines, and sub-dividing the land to build eighteen new homes. As a licensed realtor, I took care of the sales details.

During the first year of that business venture, we lived in an old farmhouse on the back forty acres of the property while Charles was developing the front twenty acres. The year our family lived in that old, unheated farmhouse brings back the sweetest memories of our married life.

*L to R: Uncle Mike and Anne Benton, Barbara,
brother Fred and his wife, Wanda 1958-59*

*L to R: Charles E Rowe, Jr. (Chuck),
Jeffrey Benton Rowe (Jeff) 1966-67*

*Chuck is in the driver's seat 1966-67*

*Chuck and Jeff Rowe 1970-71*

*Charles with Duke (Great Dane) 1966-67*

*Barbara riding Blue in front yard 1967-68*

"THERE AIN'T MUCH FUN IN MEDICINE, BUT THERE'S
A HECK OF A LOT OF MEDICINE IN FUN."
JOSH BILLINGS

# Chapter Three

The year was 1973, and we were living in the old farmhouse until Charles had an opportunity to design and build us a new place. Meanwhile Charles was working hard on the infrastructure of the housing development.

The farmhouse had no operating central heat system. The water source was a well drawn from a spring that was contaminated by run-off from the mountains. We boiled drinking and cooking water. One morning Charles stepped into the shower, got all soaped up, and then the pump shut off. He waited several minutes before the pressure built up enough to rinse off. Just the thought of standing in the shower in thirty degree weather waiting for that water to flow would have ruined my day—not Charles'—he came out laughing.

The U.S. was experiencing a crippling oil and gas shortage in the early seventies, and the house had been heated with propane gas. An empty storage tank sat outside, but, because of the shortage, the local gas company was not accepting new customers. We decided to grin and bear it.

After all, what's one winter without heat? That's when we learned how Ol' Man Winter could permeate concrete block houses and concrete slabs covered with vinyl tile. I would go to bed in flannel pajamas, snuggling down under several quilts, holding a book to read with gloves on my hands. Miraculously, we escaped the season's usual colds and flu. The winter was so cold that Charles kept a fire going constantly. He went into the woods, cut down trees, split logs and neatly stacked the firewood against the house.

Our family was close that winter. We hovered around the fireplace to stay warm. Charles was a wonderful storyteller, keeping us entertained with his imaginative stories. We laughed and laughed. The boys and I took turns at trying to top Charles's tall tales, but we never could match him. I remember waking up around 5:30 every morning shivering from the bitter cold of outside temperatures in the 30s. Charles rekindled the fire while I threw clothes from the washer to the dryer to add a little heat to the air. About 6:15 we woke the boys up to a slightly warmer house.

I made homemade biscuits and a hearty breakfast each morning. I loved sitting around the kitchen table talking about whatever came to mind. To me, this is what the word 'family' means. It's the kind of love that seeps into your bones.

The cold was not our only adversary. The house sat nestled in the woods about three-quarters of a mile down a dirt road that became impassable when it rained. I had renewed my real estate license that year so I could work with clients to market the new subdivision, and Charles surprised me with a new Lincoln Mark IV. Returning from work one rainy day, I drove to the end of the paved road and the beginning of the muddy, slippery, bumpy road. Before me stood the huge diesel John Deere tractor, easily two or three times the size of my car. The only way down that road to my home, other than walking, was to climb up on the John Deere and drive. Clad in a business suit, briefcase in hand, I hiked up my skirt and, with my head held high, I stepped up to the first high step and sat in the tractor seat. I hoped no one saw me as I reached for the ignition. I drove home past my spring garden and took note of how tall the vegetables had grown as they stood dancing in the rain.

***

Our preacher encouraged the church youth group to grow fresh vegetables to sell in order to generate income for the youth tours every year. At the end of high school, the group toured the four corners of the United States. Various church members hosted and planned events for national competition. Chuck even won a preaching event in Waxahachie, Texas at the competition one year.

In addition to the youth group's garden, along with our neighbors, we planted a community garden on an acre in front of our old house. One neighbor, about a mile down the main road, brought his tractor over and tilled the ground to prepare it for planting. As a way of drawing our community together, many of our neighbors in the new subdivision participated in planting and nurturing the garden. Every day we checked the garden for new growth. One afternoon, Chuck, Jeff and I went to check the garden's progress and noticed all the new corn sprouts had been pulled up. I found Charles and told him someone had vandalized the garden. When he saw the corn limply lying on the ground, he just laughed. He told me the crows had feasted in our garden. I was plain mad and didn't understand why he thought it was funny.

We replanted and I made a scarecrow to place in the garden, but about three weeks later we were robbed again by the same varmints. Once more we replanted and strung pie tins around the plants. A few weeks later—robbed again. Now I was boiling mad. We researched crows and learned they are very smart birds. In talking with neighboring farmers, we learned the best strategy for getting rid of them was to kill one and hang the corpse in the garden. We replanted and formulated our stealthy plan to assassinate one of those crows.

At the edge of the garden, armed with a sixteen-gauge shotgun, camouflaged by the tall grass, I waited—positioned to kill the first crow in sight. That first morning at six o'clock when dawn was just beginning to break, it was still and quiet, the fresh smell of the new day all around me. I could hear the sound of a crow off in the distance, coming for breakfast. "Damn crows! It'll be your last breakfast in my garden." I could hear them, but couldn't see them. It was as though they were all around the garden laughing at me. "Come on, fly over my garden, you thieving varmints," I dared them.

About seven o'clock, I walked back to the house empty-handed. Charles met me at the door with a hot cup of coffee. I handed him the shotgun to unload and vowed to go back the next day. Three more tries passed without success and Charles was finally the one who shot one of the crows. He hung it right in the middle of the garden. Those farmers knew what they were talking about. The crows abandoned the idea of plundering our garden.

Eight weeks later, we shared vegetables with neighbors who helped work it. We had a bumper crop of green beans the second year and Charles kidded about eating those beans fried, scrambled, sautéed, grilled and even in casseroles. The neighborhood shared in the bounty of corn, butter beans, squash, potatoes, carrots, lettuce, okra, tomatoes, radishes, onions and peas as well as those green beans.

\*\*\*

Chuck, now fourteen years old, started working at the country club washing clubs and charging the batteries on the golf carts. He went to the club before school every morning to drive the charged carts from the shed to the Pro Shop; after school he cleaned the clubs and drove the carts back to the shed to have their batteries charged overnight. He convinced his dad that he needed a trail bike to drive to and from work. I, the reluctant mom, insisted on safety instructions. Rule number one: Never ride without a helmet. Rule number two: Never ride in short pants.

After observing Chuck on the trail bike for a few weeks, I decided to give it a try. Charles, Chuck, Jeff and I gathered behind the old house on the dirt road. It was my turn. I mounted the bike and followed Charles' instructions to just release the gas on the handles and push *forward* to stop. Surprisingly, it took off faster than I'd planned. Wanting to stop, I pulled the handles *back* like the reins on a horse. The next thing I heard from a distance was Charles and the boys calling my name in a panic. They later told me I flew between the four-foot lawn mower attachment, the house, and an *old oak tree*. Besides, I was wearing shorts and no helmet. I was forbidden to ride Chuck's bike again.

After that incident, Chuck had his own mishap. The golf pro brought Chuck home in his arms one day. Chuck had been on his way home on the golf path and met the service truck head on. He was groggy and his forehead was soft and swollen. The doctor said he'd be okay but we should watch him through the night and not let him sleep. My best way to keep him awake was to clean out his closet. Chuck anxiously watched as I plowed through the closet sorting items into piles of discards and keepers. Lesson learned. We sold that trail bike after Chuck's wreck on the cart path.

\*\*\*

Our new home was completed in early 1974, exquisitely carved into a two-acre hillside lot, overlooking an eighty-five acre lake and the fourteenth green and fairway of Cumberland Hills Country Club. The back nine carefully winds through the foothills of the Blue Ridge Mountains. At the eighteenth tee, a golfer has to drive tee shots across a portion of the lake, or use two extra strokes playing around the edge. It was a spring-fed lake, over 100 feet deep, with water of drinking quality. This particular section was only ten to twelve feet deep. In it are a multitude of golf balls magnified by the clear water. It looks as though you could reach in and pick up as many golf balls as you could grab without getting your sleeves wet, but best not to try unless your watch is waterproof and your cap floats.

The new house had about 3,500 square feet of heated space that Charles designed just for us. Upstairs we had a living room, dining room, kitchen, master bedroom and bath, a guest room with its own bath, plus a den with a fireplace. Downstairs was a second den with a fireplace and a wet bar flanked by two bedrooms with baths for the boys. The garage had extra tall doors to store our twenty-five foot cabin cruiser and a workshop. It was a house built for privacy, with everyone having his or her own space. We didn't need to share anything; not even a bathroom. My husband kidded us by telling people he put in four thermostats, two for me and the boys to play with, and the two real ones, hidden, for him to adjust.

Charles set up a darkroom in the laundry room where he taught Chuck to develop film and print pictures. Chuck soon mastered a 35-mm camera and the darkroom. He became the school photographer. Our son, ever the entrepreneur, took pictures of the golfers on tournament day, developed the film at night and sold the pictures the next day to the winners. At school, Chuck was voted most popular and most likely to succeed. I don't know how he did all the things he did while keeping up his grades. He never presented us with a problem.

The golf course kissed our lot line one hundred feet from the back door, so we bought an electric golf cart and played eighteen holes most afternoons. Chuck and Jeff joined the swim team at the club. Jeff, now eleven, aced a hole-in-one and the Birmingham News featured his victory in the local section. Gifted with a swing that sent balls high and straight down the fairway, Jeff had dreams of becoming a pro golfer. We took golf and tennis lessons from the pro, fished in the lake and played golf at will. Jeff joined a Little League baseball team and Chuck played football. We became active in the community, but we seemed to be growing apart as a family. As he was actively involved in school, work and church functions, we rarely saw Chuck. Jeff spent a lot of time at the country club or fishing after school and on weekends. I sold real estate and kept the house running, golfed and chauffeured anyone who had to be anywhere. Life was good, but I felt something significant was fading away.

Charles worked hard; very hard. We didn't seem to find time to talk anymore. Charles not only served as a subcontractor, he worked directly with the contractors he hired. He used the surveyor's transit, setting up straight property lines and site foundations, poured concrete, erected the frames, cleaned up the construction sites and laid brick with the brick masons. He even helped painters and roofers. Late in the afternoons, after a short rest, he worked on our one and a half acre yard. I cannot remember one single complaint. At night he ordered materials for the next day and scheduled workers for the upcoming phase of construction. For pleasure, he enjoyed talking on his ham radio late at night. Charles possessed an enormous gift of gab. I am shy about talking to people I don't know, so one night when he asked me to talk to a fellow in Ireland, all I could think to ask was, "How's the weather?"

Soon our beautiful home became just a house. I vacuumed and cleaned and cleaned and vacuumed, swabbing one bathroom after another. Charles became stressed when another economic recession hit. Our new houses stopped selling. He told us to cut back on expenses at the country club. One day Chuck came home upset because the neighborhood gas station had confiscated his gas card. Charles had told us expenses were tight, but the bill was two or three months past due. As a family, we were drifting apart. We didn't even watch TV together anymore. Charles spent most of his evenings talking on the ham radio. Chuck and I grew closer with church activities, but Jeff stayed home with his dad. While my husband claimed to get more out of listening to gospel music than going to church, I needed the support of my church family. I attended twice on Sunday and again during the week. My husband felt neglected and told me I was a poor excuse for a Christian. That hurt!

I talked to my minister who asked me, "How do you put church, God and family in proper order?"

"God, family, then church," I replied with tears in my eyes.

"Then you already know the right answer. How else can I help you?" he asked. I thought about that answer a lot, then vowed to myself to never enter a church again unless we all walked in together. Indeed, it was the mid-1990s before I walked back into a church—alone.

*North End of House 1970's*

## *Chapter Four*

T he entrepreneurial spirit in Charles was still strong. Another recession had hit and the real estate development in Birmingham was
fading, so it was time to begin again. His brother-in-law in Florida wanted
him to come down and head up a new housing development near Orlando.
Charles left for this new opportunity the day after Christmas in 1978. I
adamantly told him I would never move to Florida.

Our family was divided. Chuck was a senior in high school. Jeff had
a girlfriend. And I did not want to leave our life behind. Charles went to
Florida and lived with his sister and brother-in-law. We all cried. Jeff became defiant. He point-blank refused to consider moving and warned us
of dire consequences if we forced the issue. While I was visiting Charles in
Florida, Chuck and Jeff got into a fight at home and Jeff rammed his fist
through a wall. I didn't know how to handle behavior like that.

Chuck graduated from high school the following June and went to
Florida to visit his dad. While there, he found a job selling cars, moved out
of our house and settled into an apartment. That left Jeff and me alone

in the big house. I continued with my real estate job and sold some of the houses Charles had built. My zeal to work with people was gone; I didn't want to cook; I didn't want to play golf. I sat—lifeless in a lifeless house.

Jeff began having more and more problems. He was out of my control, refusing to come home when I told him to. He began smoking pot and hanging out with people I didn't know anything about. He was accused of wrecking several golf carts at the country club. I dropped him at the skating rink one night and later received a call from the police that Jeff had been arrested for waving a bag of pot in the air while out on a street corner. I was really scared; as I drove to the jail to pick him up, I prayed. I didn't know how I was going to deal with this. Feeling sick at my stomach as I got into the car, I remember praying, "God I can't handle this...I'm moving over! You drive!" When I called Charles about these incidents, he told me it was something I was going to have to deal with on my own. I made two or three trips to visit him in Florida, and, later in the year, I finally told him I would put the house up for sale and move there. I had to get help with Jeff. I wasn't willing to lose my son and not do anything to stop it.

Tears in my eyes, memories and images in my head, I reluctantly climbed into the U-Haul that took us into a fifteen-year nightmare. Just a year earlier I had told my husband I would never move to Florida, and yet, here I was, doing that very thing. As we drove away, our fifteen-year-old son Jeff threatened, "I'll make you and Dad regret making me move." That statement was chilling. As I gave our home one last look, I tried to analyze what had gone wrong.

***

We bought a condo in Maitland, Florida. Our home in Alabama didn't sell, so we rented it out. Charles was again working hard to make the new housing development a success. I obtained a Florida real estate license and handled the sale of the homes.

Now living in Florida, Jeff was completely uncontrollable, and I used every avenue I could find to plead for help. I looked in the yellow pages and began calling agencies, only to be told that unless Jeff was willing to accept help, there was nothing they could do for us. We didn't know who his friends were. If we sent him to his room, he would go out the window and be gone for two or three days, cutting school.

Though we knew about his marijuana use, we didn't have any knowledge of the use of more potent drugs. As far as we knew, he wasn't using alcohol. It seemed to be a matter of pure rebellion.

His girlfriend, Dawn, called us late one night and said, "Come down to the hospital. Jeff ran his hand through a sliding glass door and is cut." Charles and I jumped in the car and raced to the emergency room. I pulled the doctor aside and told him, "Our son's messing with drugs, and we don't know what to do…even what he's on. Please do a drug or urine test and let us know, so we know what we're dealing with." The doctor ran the tests and told us he had marijuana and Quaaludes in his system. I had to look up Quaaludes to see what they were.

There seemed to be nowhere to turn for help. I looked to God for the strength and wisdom to make the right decisions. Our family had not joined a church in Florida, but Charles's sister and brother-in-law were members of the Baptist church. I went to the youth minister there to ask his advice. Charles didn't go with me for the consultation. He thought this was just a "stage" Jeff would outgrow. The youth minister asked what Jeff liked to do. Jeff had always excelled in golf and was an excellent player with a beautiful, natural swing, and he loved the game. The minister told us he would invite Jeff to play a round of golf in the hope of starting a meaningful conversation. Unfortunately, that golf game was never to be.

"SECURITY IS MOSTLY A SUPERSTITION. IT DOES NOT EXIST
IN NATURE, NOR DO THE CHILDREN OF MEN,
AS A WHOLE, EXPERIENCE IT."
HELEN KELLER

# Chapter Five

Jeff was employed part-time at a printing center near our condo. Charles thought we could keep a better eye on him if he and Jeff worked together on the construction site, so Jeff began working for his dad, cleaning up the home sites, picking up wood and other debris. I became worried that if Charles paid Jeff in cash, he would use the money to buy drugs. I wanted to be sure we were not playing a part in his drug use so I suggested Charles let him know we would save his pay and give him the money when he was willing to straighten himself out. The date was July 25, 1980. Charles and Jeff had a huge argument about the money, and Jeff stormed off the construction lot.

That same night Jeff was killed in a high speed auto wreck. He got into a friend's car; the driver had been drinking. As they raced with another car, they sideswiped the other vehicle. The car Jeff was riding in flipped and crashed. He was thrown over the seat and his chest was crushed. Our sixteen-year-old son was dead. The driver walked away without a scratch.

At the hospital that night Charles's face was drained of all color, and I told him, "Charles, don't blame yourself for this. This is not your fault." I could tell he felt if he'd only given Jeff the money, this would never have happened. I was heartsick and numb with pain. I asked God over and over—'WHY? What have I done so wrong?'

Though faith and friends are what get us through times like these, it is so hard to respond to encouraging words, to tell the story over and over. After a few weeks, as I was visiting the cemetery, I found a way to express what I was feeling and to tell friends of our gratitude for their caring. At the cemetery, I wrote this letter to many of those who had given us such loving support. The letter is dated August 9, 1980—a few weeks after the accident:

> *Dear Friends,*
>
> *There is a huge oak tree here at the cemetery. Jeff's friends tied a big yellow ribbon around the tree the day after the funeral. The cemetery is about three miles from where we live. We bought four plots instead of one—if we move back to Birmingham someday, we'll have Jeff moved too. He always wanted to go home. I chose the spot under this tree where the oak can shade him under its abundant leaves. There are lots of squirrels and birds out here, but everything looks flat. Only flat grave markers are allowed. We have one with a vase for flowers, but they are only allowed on holidays and birthdays. The kids, his friends, called Jeff "Alabama" down here. Someone started to carve 'Bama' in the tree, but there is only 'Bam.' I guess somebody from the cemetery ran them off before they could do the 'a.' I bet they will come back and finish.*
>
> *I can't believe this is happening. Each day gets harder and darker and the reality is hard to bear. Jeff said he'd make us regret moving him to Florida. He has had so many narrow escapes this past year, as*

*if God were trying to warn him. Jeff died instantly in the crash. The accident report said his heart was lacerated; his breastbone crushed. The car lost control, hit a tree, turned over and slid upside down for about 600 feet. They must have been going more than 100 miles per hour. The preliminary report said 'speed unknown.'*

*We have heard the second car involved belongs to four or five different people. The police and investigators will not talk to us about it. Charles has been doing some investigating on his own. The police have both cars hidden. Charles and Chuck did see the car Jeff was in. It had taken the police twenty minutes to cut Jeff out of the car. He was pinned between the top of the seat and the roof of the car. The accident was on the news, but I couldn't watch it. Charles and Chuck watched and said the rescue squad was beating on Jeff's chest. I couldn't stand that. Jeff's girlfriend Dawn called about 2:30 a.m. on Saturday and asked how Jeff was. She must have assumed we had been notified, but we didn't know what she was talking about. She told us, "Jeff's been in a terrible accident and it's bad—I know it's bad—they were beating on his chest and I couldn't get to him! Please come and get me. I don't have a way to get to the hospital."*

*We dressed quickly and picked Dawn up on the way. Charles went in to the emergency entrance. I parked the car and Dawn and I walked almost two blocks from the parking lot to the hospital. When I walked in, Charles looked pale. He said, "Honey, he's D.O.A."*

*I cried out, "No! How do they know it was Jeff! How do they know it was Jeff!" I knew he had no I.D. I pleaded with the doctor, "How do you know it's Jeff?" The doctor told me they identified him by his driver's license.*

*Dawn was the one who went back to identify him. She was hysterical and she confirmed that it was Jeff. He had Chuck's driver's license on him—that had gone missing a few days before.*

*All I could see at that moment was Jeff meeting Jesus—he met Jesus! He was walking around in heaven meeting Mother and Daddy, grandparents and Aunt Lillian. His life wasn't over; it was just beginning. Satan took our son away from us but God took over and made things beautiful. When we took Dawn home she told me, "Thank you, Mrs. Rowe. I'll remember what you said."*

*We planned a service to give glory to God and try to make something positive out of this tragedy. When Dawn asked if she and another friend could come, we told her to ask all Jeff's friends to come—that it would help us. We wanted them to have this mean something to them and to walk in the way of Jesus. Several of them made the decision to live for Christ. Now if they will only follow through. We asked them to call us if they needed help. They couldn't believe we didn't hate them for what had happened. We prayed a fruitful seed was planted. These were the same friends we didn't want Jeff to be around and we wouldn't even let them come into our home. Our sister-in-law Betty went up to a boy in overalls, with big holes in his knees, who looked pitiful with tears streaming down his face. She put her arms around him and told him she loved him. He asked, "How can you love me when I helped kill Jeff? Betty replied, "Because Jesus loves you through me."*

*Now I'm beginning to feel the deep pain of knowing Jeff isn't going to ever walk back in again—ever. Charles says to think about the path Jeff was on before he was killed and how God permitted Satan, in a way, to help save him. How ironic! I can't help being selfish sometimes and wanting my son back—good times or bad. Another part of my heart has been ripped away, but damn Satan will never rule over me. I feel like ants are crawling over me and eating me alive, inside and out. There's nowhere to turn to get rid of them except to lie still and know God has me in His control. At times I have trouble lying still and being patient. Oh I wish it had been me getting to go to heaven! Do I have to stay here till I am 100 years old? Today I am in the pits of self-pity. Jeff is lying under this oak tree and I am pouring my heart out writing this.*

*Jeff once nursed an orphaned baby red-headed woodpecker for about two weeks, feeding him, trying to make him comfortable and loving him. He dug up worms for the baby bird to eat, but the bird eventually died. Charles told me the first time he came out to the cemetery this oak tree was full of woodpeckers and he felt it was God's way of letting him know Jeff was okay. I have thought about taking Jeff home to Birmingham, but Charles says he couldn't stand leaving Jeff up there with us living so far away. He said if we ever move back, Jeff will go with us.*

*Another storm in life has come and gone and there is peace now—God's peace. We'll pick up the pieces and prepare for the next battle. We are okay, I think, and we thank you for your prayers and love and thoughtfulness. I am blessed to have friends to help me and my family walk through this dark moment. The cards and letters I read over and over. The phone calls and flowers mean so much to me. I have needed you and you have not let me down. I will be here for you always…*

\*\*\*

Life can hurt a lot. I lifted Jeff up to Jesus and thank Him for the short time we had together. Jeff was with Mother, Daddy, Grandmother and Cap. They were together in a better place. At times my heart wished and even asked God why Jeff had to be the one to die and not any of the other kids in the accident that night. Though I was devastated by Jeff's death, I continued to be strong for my family because that was how I had been raised and how I had gotten through the hard, tough losses of my early years. I had to ponder the question: Why are some people stronger than others when horrific tragedies occur? Just like the roots of that mighty oak tree, my roots are stout and tough. The oak's ancestors, like mine, had somehow taught it to be strong through the genetics of the centuries. I felt empowered. I would get through this with the help of God, my family and my friends.

One of the people working at the funeral home handed me a note and said, "Jeff left this for you." Through the fog of my grief, for a moment, I felt it was actually Jeff speaking to me, and the poem that follows managed to break through the heartache.

## Safely Home

I am home in heaven, dear ones;
Oh so happy and so bright.
There is perfect joy and beauty
In this everlasting light.

All the pain and grief is over,
Every restless tossing passed;
I am now at peace forever,
Safely home in heaven at last.

Did you wonder I so calmly
Trod the valley of the shade?
Oh, but Jesus' love illumined
Every dark and fearful glade.

And he came Himself to meet me
In the way so hard to tread;
And with Jesus' arm to lean on,
Could I have one doubt or dread?

Then you must not grieve so sorely,
For I love you dearly still;
Try to look beyond death's shadows,
Pray to trust our Father's will.

There is work still waiting for you,
So you must not idly stand;
Do it now while life remaineth
You shall rest in Jesus' land.

When that work is all completed,
He will gently call you home;
Oh, the rapture of that meeting,
Oh, the joy to see you come.

*Author Unknown*

*Jeff's friends speaking to Charles*
*Oak Tree in the background provides shelter*

*Jeff's friends help Barbara*

*In the upper right background is sister-in-law, Betty, who hugged*
*Jeff's broken hearted friend*

*Jeffery Benton Rowe,*
*June 11, 1964-July 25, 1980*

## *Chapter Six*

I was numb and lost. Though I was functioning and going through the routine of life, my heart was broken. Chuck went home to his apartment across town. I found I was not able to continue my work. Real estate sales is a people business, and I got out of it very quickly after Jeff's death. I couldn't make myself smile and be congenial any more. It just wasn't in my heart. I was not the person I'd been before.

I thought a lot about my relationship with Jeff over the last few years of his life…how we didn't approve of his friends and the path he seemed to be pursuing. I even used to fuss at him about his long hair. If only I could have him back, I would comb that hair for him every day. I'd even roll it up and braid it if he wanted me to. I used to think losing my parents had been my worst nightmare, but this was a desolation almost impossible to bear.

We received $50,000 from an insurance company for Jeff's death. A buddy Charles worked with played a list of numbers at jai alai games, a popular sport in Florida at the time. Charles had the list and told me he was going to play. I tried to talk him out of it, but he insisted he knew what he was doing and said I shouldn't worry. Charles took that insurance money and began betting on jai alai games and lost it all. I believe the gambling was a symptom of his grieving process.

I knew I had to find a job—not just for the money, but to keep me sane. I went to a class to learn to type so I could get out into the job market. Just out of typing class and having no idea what I was capable of doing, I had to find out where I fit into the workplace. My first job was with Kelly Temporary Services where they sent me on a six-week assignment at United Telephone of Florida (later bought out by Sprint Corporation). United Telephone hired me for a permanent position after the temp assignment was over. The job was a distraction from home problems, provided a sense of filling up my brain with other matters and a way of making some friends. It was a daily relief from a marriage that was not going the way I would have hoped and the effort of trying to hold on to my own sanity.

Several years passed and Charles seemed to be ambling through life with no direction. His heart was broken. After losing Jeff, he never built another house. To acquire some cash, he bought items at flea markets and resold them. Once in a while he took the boat out for a charter excursion. My income paid the bills. Charles began drinking quite a bit. He never got over Jeff's death.

Looking back over a three-decade marriage, I knew the girl I had been when Charles married me was not the woman I had become. We had grown so far apart. If Charles had married someone else, he might have had a better marriage. He couldn't seem to come to terms with losing Jeff. Though he didn't have those *strong oak tree roots* that my parents instilled in me, he was a man who felt emotion deeply, and he visited the cemetery where our son was buried to cling to the same strength of that mighty tree. When his aunt and uncle lost their son, we gifted them with some small *oak trees* and Charles wrote them a heartfelt note which, I think, revealed his own pain:

*Dear Aunt Rea and Uncle Odell,*

*The oak tree is symbolic of strength; the kind of strength that Wayne had. People have been known to even strap themselves to such a tree in order to survive the winds of a storm. To me, the tree is also symbolic of love. It shades you in the summer and then sheds its leaves in winter to let the sun rays give you warmth. The trees are so mighty, yet humble. They cast their small seeds upon the ground so that future generations will grow and carry on.*

*Please accept these oaks and plant them in a special place where you can watch them grow and enjoy them. And, remember, a part of Wayne will always be there in the seeds he cast…his children, grand-children, and on and on.*

*I have my special place to reminisce, talk, cry, laugh a little, and remember the good times I had with my lost loved ones. My special place that gives me so much comfort is a very special oak tree.*

*With love and understanding… Charles*

\*\*\*

I enrolled at Rollins College and began taking courses with the goal of getting a degree in Accounting. At long last, I was pursuing my college education. When Rollins College discontinued the Accounting major, I switched to an Organizational Communications major with an emphasis in Public Relations.

Without warning, Charles informed me he was going to open a pawn-shop and was getting a second mortgage on the still-unsold house in Birmingham to finance the start-up. Charles loved cameras and tools. He opened the pawnshop stocked predominately with construction tools and

35mm cameras, plus the items he'd been purchasing at garage sales and flea markets.

I was very much against the pawnshop. I felt it was a highly dangerous business and tried to talk him out of it. We grew further apart. We were living under the same roof, but not connecting very much. He began accusing me of all sorts of strange behavior. Our marriage had sunk to a seriously low point.

Pre-occupied with my failing marriage, I was not prepared for the next explosion in my life.

***

Our son, Chuck, visited me one day and broke the unbearable news that he had contracted the AIDS virus. This was incomprehensible. How could this be happening?

Stunned, I asked him if he was a homosexual, and he said, "No, Mom, I'm not." He broke down and cried. I had never considered that possibility, and I wondered if he contracted HIV through a blood transfusion or a female partner. In the end it didn't matter.

"It doesn't make any difference how you got this. You're my son, I love you and I'll see you through it," was my response.

After a few months, he came home to live with us. His medication cost about $1,200 a month. Charles refused to help pay for any of it, saying it wouldn't help anyway. That was the breaking point for me—you don't say those hopeless words to a mother. I would do whatever had to be done to help my son. I prayed and believed a cure was just right around the corner. My husband still called our place home, but he spent his nights on a cot at the pawnshop. We saw very little of him.

Chuck told me, "Mom, you need to get a divorce. You deserve better than this. Get on with your life and find someone else."

I made an appointment with a divorce attorney recommended by one of my co-workers at Sprint. After we talked, the attorney said, "I have a doctor I want you to talk to—a psychologist. Don't be alarmed, but she might put you in the hospital for a few days." That scared me to death. I stopped at a pay phone on my way home and called her, Dr. Debbie Douglas at Psychological Associates, and made the appointment.

Dr. Douglas looked so young, I could not imagine she could help me, but she became an amazing positive force in my troubled life. When I told her the attorney thought she might put me in the hospital, she laughed. I must have frightened him so much that he wanted to direct me straight to someone who could keep me from going over the edge.

Debbie and I talked at length. I told her about Jeff's death and about my struggling marriage. She brought up the subject of something called Battered Woman Syndrome. I responded with what I truly believed at the time, "I'm not battered; Charles has never hit me. Something's wrong with *me*; *I'm* the one who needs to be fixed."

I was finally taking steps toward recovering my own spirit. I took Chuck with me to see Debbie. I started attending a support group for battered women that Debbie facilitated. There I found there's more than one way to be 'battered.' Breaking down of a spouse's spirit and sense of self-worth can be just as damaging. I know Charles never meant to do psychological damage to me, but he was a man of his time and belief system. I also joined a support group for HIV/AIDS. The AIDS group seemed like a good networking opportunity to find avenues to get the help and medication Chuck needed. Debbie guided me through all of this. She recommended a divorce attorney who would work within my limited budget and I filed for divorce. I arranged for the divorce papers to be sent to Charles at the pawnshop. I had gained enough confidence in myself to take the necessary steps to move on with life. While my co-workers knew little about my private life, my job was therapeutic as a means of emotional support.

The concern of family and friends is key to recovering after a loss. For many years I had been estranged from my brother Freddy. He cut himself off from the entire Benton family after his second marriage, including me and our Aunt Lillian. At first I would call him, crying, asking what I had done, and he would hang up on me. In late fall of 1990, after years of estrangement, Freddy called me to reconnect. I was so touched and happy to hear from him at that burdensome moment in my life, I never even asked him what had been the cause of his distancing himself from the family.

Freddy asked me to join him and his third wife for a weekend in Miami before they embarked on a cruise. I was thrilled to accept the invitation. They put me up in a beautiful hotel with a breathtaking view of the water. The best part of that weekend was walking on the dock with my brother, holding his hand and just being with him. Through tears of joy, my heart was lifted and I felt energized with a renewed spirit and the strength to face my next test…caring for my dying son.

I had no idea a different shattering event would intervene to transform my life.

*Photo Taken 1991*
*Charles E. Rowe, Jr.,*
*August 10, 1961-November 17, 1993*

"PRAYER IS NOT ASKING. IT IS A LONGING OF THE SOUL. IT IS DAILY ADMISSION OF ONE'S WEAKNESS.IT IS BETTER IN PRAYER TO HAVE A HEART WITHOUT WORDS THAN WORDS WITHOUT A HEART."
MAHATMA GANDHI

# *Chapter Seven*

The divorce papers were delivered to Charles at the pawnshop in early May, 1992. He had put a cot in the back of the shop and spent his days working behind the counter and nights sleeping in the back.

On May 14, 1992, a shop employee showed up for work before the scheduled 9 a.m. opening time and found Charles lying dead on the floor behind the counter in a pool of his own blood. He had been shot multiple times; blood spatter was everywhere. Since no signs of a forced entry were evident it was assumed he had recognized his assailants and buzzed them into the store some time after closing the night before. He had been known to open the door if a customer he recognized knocked after closing time. Also, the video tape had been torn out of the security camera.

Pawnshop owners are aware they are in a dangerous business. Pawnbrokers lend cash and display valuables and are frequently robbery targets because of that. Charles was an expert shot. He had four guns lying on the counter and under the counter was a button he could press to send an alarm directly to the police department. Even with that intense security, he had been shot eight times. The police surmised he was taken by surprise as the men engaged him in conversation at the counter. There were no signs of a struggle. The only damage was a broken jewelry case, so it was apparent the killers shot him fairly quickly and grabbed what they wanted before fleeing the scene.

I was at work that morning when a detective phoned me and said something like, "I hate to tell you this, but your husband has committed suicide." A cold chill ran through me–as if someone had doused me with ice cold water.

"Committed suicide?" I questioned.

"Yes," he said, and proceeded to apologize for breaking the news over the phone. He asked if we had argued on the day of the murder and if we argued often. I replied that we argued any time Charles did not get his way.

I was desperate to get home to our son. I didn't know if the police had called Chuck before they called me. I told my boss, "I've got to go. Charles committed suicide last night."

Linda, one of my friends at work said, "I'm going with you."

"No," I told her. "No you're not. I'm fine."

I left the office alone and Linda knocked on my door a few minutes after I got home. She said, "I'm just going to sit, not going to talk to you, just going to sit and answer the phone for you."

She did that and it turned out to be a blessing. I was unaware at the time, but this was not a suicide—it was a high profile murder case. As soon as the news media began calling, I discovered Charles had not killed himself, but had been murdered. Chuck went down to the pawnshop to try to find out what was going on.

Police officers never came to ask me any questions or clarify the reason for the suicide story they gave me over the phone. I was virtually paralyzed by shock and fear. I eventually asked the investigating detective directly why he had told me it was a suicide. He only shrugged and said he didn't remember, and I didn't pursue the question. After the two kill-ers were caught, I was asked if I had any connection with them. I believe the detective may have been probing me for signs of being involved in a murder plot—thus the questions about whether or not my husband and I ever argued.

From media stories on television and the newspaper, Chuck and I found out Charles had been shot multiple times between 6 and 9 p.m. the previous evening, and a jewelry display case was smashed, with some of the jewelry missing. The local news stations kept calling the house and wanting an interview. Thank goodness for Chuck who handled all of the immediate media contact. He was the one who was interviewed.

My husband and I had been married for 32 years. Charles was a good person and I loved him, but we had drifted apart. My heart ached for the good times we'd had together and the joys and sorrows we'd shared. My minister from Birmingham, Lou and his wife, Alice, flew to Florida to preside over Charles's funeral. It was touching that Lou and Alice came all that way to be there for me. I had always been worried about the dangers of the pawnshop business, but I knew Charles had no regrets. It was what he wanted to do.

At the funeral, business neighbors and fellow pawnbrokers remem-bered Charles as a soft-spoken, gentle man. A columnist for the *Orlando Sentinel,* who was a customer of the shop, wrote a beautiful tribute column about him for the newspaper. In the meantime, I tried to cope with my feelings. Charles was dead; Chuck was dying. Thankfully, God was my best friend through all of this.

I didn't go to the shop right away, but eventually went there after ev-erything had been cleaned up. Because state law mandates that a pawnshop remains open for at least sixty days so customers will have an opportunity to buy back their pawned goods, Chuck and I were legally required to re-sume the business. I was scared to death and sat in the back room most of the time. In a state of intense anxiety, I was never afraid of the murderers; I was in shock, frightened of the pawnshop and the evil aura it carried, worried and wondering, 'what will I do now?' I hired an off-duty policeman to stand at the door the whole time I was in the shop. I did what I was legally mandated to do, giving customers those few weeks to come and buy back their pawned items. The hired officer was there every day and followed me when I made the daily bank deposit. No one seemed to understand my terror, and I couldn't explain it. I was petrified of the whole sordid business; it just wasn't my world.

The police caught the two boys who did this a week or two afterward. They were 19 and 21 years old, and one of them had been a regular customer at the shop. They shot my husband to death just so he would not be able to identify them. The two were caught when they pawned some of the stolen jewelry at a nearby shop. They confessed to the crime. The arrests answered my prayers and did a lot to ease my fears.

After things calmed down, I told the Assistant District Attorney, Mary Ann Clem, there were several video tapes from the pawnshop that I had taken home with me to watch at a later date. She strongly suggested that I not watch the tapes without her being present. She was afraid the murder may have been recorded, and she didn't want me to see the crime when I was alone. Such a tape would have been valuable prosecutorial evidence as well. A few days later she came to the condo and we watched the videos together, but the actual murder did not appear on any of the tapes. Remembering my husband's feelings about women in the workplace, I mused about how ironic it was that a 'girl' was the prosecutor on his case.

Ms. Clem asked me an abrupt question, "How do you want to see the outcome of this trial?"

I was surprised by the question. "I want you to carry out your job," was my reply. I just couldn't bring myself to answer any other way. I felt like I would be murdering somebody if I pressed for the death penalty. I wanted her to carry out the law to its fullest extent, but I wasn't going to tell her I wanted those boys killed. Troubled, I called Lou, my minister in Birmingham.

"Lou," I asked, "how would you have answered that question if Alice had been murdered?"

He said, "Well, if I couldn't shoot them myself, I'd want them to spend life in prison because the death penalty would be way too easy."

His reply brought a smile to my face and showed the basic humanity of this good friend and minister. I thought that reasoning sounded pretty good, so the next time I talked with Ms. Clem, I told her I wanted them in prison for life.

The younger perpetrator testified against his partner, in exchange for an agreement with prosecutors to not seek the death penalty. Because the two boys had confessed, there was no trial to determine guilt or innocence. What is known as the penalty phase of the sentencing shows mitigating and aggravating factors to determine an appropriate sentence. This process lasted two or three days. Chuck was quite ill by then and only able to attend one half-day session. Our nephew James attended one session. Most of the time, on my side of the courtroom sat only Dr. Debbie, the victim advocate, and me. The other side of the courtroom was packed with the murderers' families and friends. I had rarely even seen the inside of a courtroom before this and now I had to come face-to-face with two cold-blooded murderers. I had never felt so alone. Terrified. Dr. Debbie had diagnosed my fears as acute anxiety and debilitating distress. I have no words to explain how frightened I was. What was I doing here?

The trial proceeded on to the sentencing phase. Charles's sister, Syble, came from her home in South Carolina to join me. The judge wanted to listen to the victims' rights statements we had prepared. Syble read hers. The judge struck several sentences from the record. I read mine. The judge struck most of it.

That night I phoned a judge in Orange County, and told him how anguished we felt after the Seminole County judge took our victims' rights statements apart. He advised me to tell the judge we were going to give our statements as written, based on Florida law protecting victims' rights. After standing in court and demanding my rights, I walked to the ladies' room and broke down sobbing from the stress. My sister-in-law came into the restroom, and we stood together crying and holding one another. It is out of character for me to break down, and Syble told me it was the first time she had ever seen me cry.

The younger murderer received a life sentence without the possibility of parole for twenty-five years. There were also additional years added to the sentence for robbery and for firing a weapon inside a building. The older man avoided the death sentence, but was sentenced to back-to-back life sentences and would not be eligible for parole for fifty-plus years. He was also convicted of the two lesser charges and received additional prison time for those offenses.

Those prison sentences did not ease the pain I felt. They couldn't erase the memories nor replace a father's unconditional love for his son who was fighting an uphill battle against a terrible illness. The murderers will be housed, fed and clothed, ironically, on my tax dollars. They will have medical attention and have access to a college education. The irony continues. The older murderer, since he has been in prison, has gotten married and now has children through conjugal visits with his wife. He comes up for parole every five years or so and pleads to be released. I go to Tallahassee for every parole hearing to give a victim's statement. The younger one is eligible to be out in 25 years from the beginning of his sentence, a date which is coming up in only a few years. He will be 45 years old then and will have another chance at life. My husband was not given a chance for even one more day. He did not even have the chance to defend himself. The families of crime victims receive no help with medical attention, counseling, education, housing or food. They are robbed of their loved ones forever and of any emotional and financial support their loved ones could provide over a lifetime.

For a while after the trial, I was angry at God. I could not understand or comprehend my life of tragedies. Why me? What was I supposed to do? One woman actually came up to me saying, "You must have done something in your life to deserve this." I didn't know what I could have done that would be so bad. Later I heard a preacher on the radio say, "God doesn't sit in heaven and cause tragedies. He doesn't say 'I think I'll crash that teen-agers car, or give that woman cancer, or give that man a heart attack so that his widow learns a lesson.' He doesn't cause these things to happen. If He did, He couldn't be my God. We have a free will to make choices, and God doesn't make these things happen." It was a moment of reality for me. I knew then that God doesn't create these tragedies. Life is made up of choices. In my life going forward, I could choose the path of positive strength or negative weakness. I chose to be strong and to meet my next challenge head on.

***

Because there was such a stigma attached to the disease in the 1990s, Chuck didn't want anyone to know that he had AIDS and made me promise not to tell the truth about his condition. This was very upsetting for me, and I was worried about his friends' safety, and felt they needed to know about his condition, but I kept my promise. He told everyone he had cancer. He was so desperate to keep his diagnosis hidden, he even threatened to sue me if I revealed it to anyone. We had some serious talks about this, but he was adamant.

As Chuck's health declined, I took him on two Caribbean cruises. We enjoyed the restful atmosphere and the meditation value of the sparkling ocean, but it was a struggle to give myself over to the tranquility of the voyage, knowing what was happening to my beloved son. We took part in cruise activities as much as Chuck's health and energy would allow. He was trying to live out some of his life wishes.

Chuck was very ill and, without discussing it with me, he used some of the money Charles had left him and rented an apartment of his own. He furnished his new place and bought a used Corvette. I know he was trying to have a last fling at life, but he was back home with me within six weeks.

Chuck was all I had left…and he was terminally ill. For about a year, he only had the HIV virus, but it took a while to become advanced. By the time of the murder and the sentencing hearing, his illness had advanced to full-blown AIDS. Because of the HIPAA patient privacy laws, I could not talk to any of the doctors about his condition even though I tried. Chuck needed me, and I wanted to be there for him so I took training to learn how to care for him and administer his medication by injection. I was going to the AIDS support groups to find out how we could get help. I learned which pharmacists could and would help with getting the drugs at lower costs. I networked with others about the illness. When you're caring for someone with advanced AIDS, there is no thinking…there is only do-ing. We hired a registered nurse for Chuck who came once a week at first. Mentally and physically exhausted, I next hired a live-in caregiver to do the cooking and help with Chuck's care.

Dr. Debbie helped me make the decision to back away from my full time caregiver role, saying, "Barbara, you need to be a mom again. Chuck is not letting you do that right now."

It was best that I leave. I didn't want to be the one who seemed to be trying to stop him from any enjoyment he might get out of his final weeks and months. The nurse would come in a few times a week and the care-giver would be there to handle the day-to-day situation, so when I came by to visit I could be the loving and supportive mom I wanted to be. I appreciated Debbie helping me to make that decision.

Kathy, a good friend of mine who lived across the street, also felt I needed to get into a new environment. I knew new surroundings would help me to survive and to catch my breath. The four of us Rowe's had lived in the same condo as a family since 1979. Kathy and her husband literally moved me to another condo on a lake only two blocks away. I rented the unit while it was up for sale with the stipulation that it could be shown to prospective buyers. Chuck remained at my place and was managing pretty well, with help from the caregivers. From the balcony of my new place, I could watch the Rollins College rowing team working out on the lake when I awoke each morning. I remember thinking metaphorically about keeping my oars in the water, staying strong and rowing through my life.

I want to remember Chuck as he was before he was ravaged by this terrible illness. The end of AIDS is not peaceful or pretty. He passed away about a year and a half after Charles was murdered. When he died I put in the obituary that he had died of AIDS. I kept my promise to him while he was alive, but I couldn't continue without telling the truth after his death.

Though I hadn't yet joined a church in Florida, I had started going to the Presbyterian Church near where I was living, and I asked that minister to preside at Chuck's funeral. It was a small and simple graveside service.

*** 

The accumulated stress of being caught up in the legal system with estate attorneys, the prosecution of my husband's murderers, handling of business affairs and the effects of dealing with Chuck's final illness, led to some physical repercussions. Anxiety is one of my enemies; high blood pressure is another. Depression tried to creep in and fear of the unknown was trapping me when I least expected it. I learned to take one day at a time and strive for a life of my own while trying hard to cherish the good times and not dwell on the bad. Often, though, I found myself subconsciously bracing as if for an unexpected blow.

After Chuck passed away, I had the condo painted and tore out and replaced the carpet with tile. It was still familiar, but freshened up, some of the memories seemed less pervasive. I rented it out to my niece, Sheila, for a time after her divorce. Some time passed and my source of funds was dwindling so that I could no longer afford to rent a separate dwelling place. When the place I was renting finally sold, I had to move; it was time for me to re-occupy the space where I had lived with my family for so many years. I reluctantly asked Sheila to move out, and I moved back into my own condo.

My family was gone. Again. Even my brother Freddy had by now passed away. I had always thought I would be a grandmother by this time of my life. I went back to work, trying to pick up the pieces of my shattered life. I needed to know God was at my side. The poem called *Footprints In The Sand* helped to express my thoughts.

## Footprints In The Sand
Author Unknown

One night I had a dream...I dreamed
I was walking along the beach
with the Lord and across the sky flashed
scenes from my life. For each scene I
noticed two sets of footprints in the sand.
One belonged to me and the other to the Lord.
When the last scene of my life flashed
before us, I looked back at the footprints in
the sand. I noticed that many times along
the path of my life, there was only one
set of footprints.
I also noticed that it happened at the very
lowest and saddest times in my life. This
really bothered me, and I questioned the
Lord about it. "Lord, you said that once I
decided to follow you, you would walk with
me all the way; but I have noticed that
during the most troublesome times in my
life, there is only one set of footprints. I
don't understand why in times when I
needed you the most, you should leave me."
The Lord replied, "My precious, precious
child. I love you and I would never, never
leave you during your times of trial and
suffering. When you saw only one set of
footprints, it was then that I carried you."

Anger is a crippling emotion, sapping energy that should be directed toward healing. I found wisdom in an article I discovered in a March, 2014 publication called *VOCAL (Victims of Crime and Leniency) Newsletter*. It is partially reprinted here with permission of the author:

### Counselor's Corner
### Anger Has a Voice

### *By LaTonya Coleman*

Anger has a voice…it always has. The voice of anger sometimes gives birth to tears, sometimes it is quiet and withdrawn, sometimes it is loud, sometimes it yells, sometimes it screams, sometimes it cries. At other times it's like a consuming ball of fire deep in the core of our souls jumping out through tears, misguided actions, and poor word choices we are unable to retract. I suspect the voice of anger ignited many of the historical events we read about in our history books…

In our personal lives, losing a loved one may contribute to anger sprouting up in our hearts and our minds. Anger without direction or understanding can lead to poor health, heart attack, stroke, lack of sleep, migraines, frustration and lack of progress in our personal lives. Anger is a human emotion that is corrosive in nature; it doesn't go away when we release it. We must learn to redirect the anger to a positive place and learn to cope with the emotion so that we may live a positive life and honor the loss of our loved ones through celebrating the life they once had here on earth.

Anger is a combination of pleasure, happiness and pain. The pleasure is in loving our family member and knowing them intimately, mixed with the pain of not having them in our physical presence any longer. We cope with the loss by placing energy and thoughts on the positive loving side of knowing and demonstrate it through looking at a photo or eating at their favorite restaurant, once we are strong enough to accept the loss and recognize it as a meaningful loss. Then once we accept the loss as meaningful, we can take small steps to show our love for them...

...It is okay to cry and feel saddened by the loss as it was an important part of our lives. So give your anger a resting place and honor your loved ones by acknowledging that your life was touched by their presence...

THERE ARE TIMES THE MOST PRODUCTIVE THING YOU CAN
DO IS REST. AND LET THE ANGELS WRAP YOU IN THEIR
LOVING WINGS. THEY'VE GOT YOU COVERED.
AUTHOR UNKNOWN

# *Chapter Eight*

I am fully aware I will never be what the world calls normal. At first I was like a mole sticking my head up out of the ground and retreating back into my hole. I had a totally helpless feeling. I had never had a repairman in my house. Charles or Chuck had always taken care of everything. I didn't even know how to change a thermostat. Slowly I learned to do these simple things, but I had allowed myself to become socially isolated because of my family situation. Even though I had always been a friendly person in a business sense, I had never been especially comfortable in a social setting. My family had always been the center of my universe. This was a very different world for me now. Dr. Debbie helped me through it all, even after I stopped going to the support groups I had been attending.

Grief is a process. There is an emotional reaction to deal with when a loved one is lost or during any other sort of distressing life event. Those steps are fear, anger, helplessness, insecurity, frustration of feelings of being rushed to normalcy. I spent a long time in the anger phase. For quite a while I was feeling numb and asking myself what I was going to do now.

I asked God, "Am I alive or am I dead?" I just wanted to *feel* something again. One of my co-workers was a skydiver. I told her I wanted to try it, so I hooked up a parachute and jumped out of an airplane. It was a tandem dive, where you are harnessed securely to a certified instructor who knows how to give the optimum adrenaline rush safely. The expert guides the diver through every step of the sky dive. I wanted to do something to jar me enough to let me have a *feeling*. And it sort of worked. At least I was glad I landed safely. Would I do it again? Probably not...just something I did.

I'll never forget the time I heard myself laugh for the first time. It had been so long since I heard that sound that I actually turned around to see who was laughing.

My friend Judy from Sprint asked me for a favor. "Barbara," she said, "my dad died up north and I have to get to the funeral. I'm boarding my other pets, but I have an old dog who has to have shots before he eats, drops in his eyes and has pills to take. I don't know anybody I would trust to take care of him except you. Would you mind keeping him for me for three or four days?" I said I'd be glad to. I had always had animals, but didn't have any at the time. So Judy brought her dog over. The dog had a towel he slept on, and Judy told me to spread the towel on the floor beside my bed. That night we got ready for bed, the dog got situated on his towel and as I was lying there saying my prayers, I heard the sound of breathing—labored breathing. There are no words to explain this, but it was like God infused the breath of life back into me. It was the first time I'd heard anybody or anything breathe for a long time. It seemed as though I had been dead and God was breathing spirit back into my soul. I couldn't thank Judy enough for letting me take care of that old dog. I went out and bought a Schnauzer puppy after that. Several months later, another Schnauzer pup entered my life after a neighbor needed a home for a dog she couldn't keep.

During nights when sleep eluded me, I turned to meditation techniques, using a beach scene, a mountain scene or repeating the Lord's Prayer. I had a lot of anger to deal with and going out to dinner with a friend, taking long walks to appreciate nature, enjoying a glass of wine, or writing this book all help to release some of those negative emotions.

I learned that prayer is a matter of listening as well as asking. As I navigated those rough seas, hanging on for dear life, I thought I heard God tell me, "Just stay in the boat."

Fritz, the Schnauzer puppy, was great company for me, giving me hugs, kisses and that canine unconditional love. We did a mile walk twice a day which made us both happy. I needed that happiness and a puppy is an irrational bundle of joy. He made me laugh at his antics and even at myself.

Stress begins with life situations that knock you off balance. For me it was losing a son to a drunk driver, battered woman syndrome, my husband's murder, the legal system, and my son's terrible illness and death. My situation, presented to different people, could result in different reactions. I know in my heart and my head that my husband and my sons are walking on heaven's streets of gold. Someday I will join them along with my parents and grandparents and that will be a truly happy day. My cognitive appraisal of my tragedies is not as stressful as someone who views death as a terrible, final thing.

When I was a young married woman I was confident, smart and active in my sons' school, little league football and baseball, church and swim team activities. I did things quickly and efficiently. I could cook dinner, talk on the phone and balance my checkbook all at the same time. A wellspring of endless energy propelled me through my days. After the loss of Jeff, Charles and Chuck, I lost confidence, realized I may not be so smart, and had trouble being interested in life. Mankind may mess up a lot of things, but there is beauty and tranquility in nature that I learned to appreciate.

The value of life is in the simple things, and family is the most important of all.

At the height of my grieving process, I sat down with a pencil and paper and listed the negative and positive directions I could take. I could turn to drugs or alcohol or suicide on the negative side, or I could continue with my education and try to use my tragedies in some sort of positive way. To some it may have seemed easier to sit at home alone with a bottle of wine each evening full of self-pity, but I was determined to make a good choice, and God was nudging me in that direction.

I wasn't angry at God anymore. I know He is a loving God and doesn't wish evil on His children. I felt He had something in mind for me to do with my life. Often, tragic outcomes are a matter of bad choices. In my family situation, Jeff should not have been fooling with those drugs. He never should have gotten in the car with the driver who had been drinking. Charles never should have opened the pawnshop. As for Chuck, I don't know how he got AIDS, but whatever choice he'd made, he was my son and I loved him completely.

I set up a meeting with my new minister, showed him all of the newspaper articles about my family and said, "This is me. I know God wants me to do something and obviously I am NOT getting the message. I need your help. I feel like I'm gifted. I know I can help other people going through the trauma of experiencing a loved one being murdered…of a mother losing a child…families of a loved one lost in a drunk driving tragedy… parents of a terminally ill child. I have the gift of strength. I want to know how to use it."

He said, "I want you to talk to one of our Stephen Ministry team leaders." The Stephen Ministry is a group of lay people formed to listen and be Christian friends to those going through grief. It is non-denominational and can be from any Christian church. Lay ministers go through fifty hours of training to help bring hope and healing to those in need. I went through the training and joined the Stephen Ministry at the church in 1996. It was healing for me to help others.

Stephen Ministers spend an hour a week with their care receivers. It is very confidential. We let them talk, and we listen as Christian friends. We don't profess to have answers, but pray with them. We aren't there as ministers, but as friends and confidants. Often the people in a particular situation cannot unburden themselves to those around them without jeopardizing their situation. We aren't shocked by what they may tell us, and we don't judge them. I've sat with those who suffered from illness or abuse, those who were victims of crime or who'd suffered the loss of loved ones, as well as those who just felt more comfortable unburdening themselves to a stranger rather than their own family.

My efforts to find a useful avenue for my grief did not stop there. Still working at Sprint and taking college courses, I joined the Maitland Citizens Police Academy and the Emergency Response Team. I joined a group called STOP (Stop Turning Out Prisoners), a statewide grassroots organization designed to keep violent offenders behind bars. When a STOP representative asked if I was interested in getting involved, without hesitation, I said, "You better believe I am!"

The STOP organization was founded by Kathleen Finnegan, a former prosecutor on Florida's west coast. Her impetus for starting the group was inspired by a night of terror at the hands of a killer who was out on early release with seventeen prior arrests. She and another Assistant District Attorney, Norman Langston, were abducted at gunpoint after winning a murder indictment that afternoon. After forcing their car onto an unmarked lane and robbing them of cash and jewelry, the killer began shooting. Attempting to shield Kathleen from the bullets with his own body, Langston was killed. The killer ran off, while Finnegan, though badly wounded, managed to run for help. Giving up her law practice, she and a local sheriff began the STOP organization a few years later to lead a drive for a Florida constitutional amendment requiring all convicted violent felons to serve at least 85 percent of their sentences.

Sprint, my employer, was so good to me. They paid my salary for two years while I did nothing but work with STOP to help keep those societal menaces locked up. The police do their part in putting the bad guys away, but the justice system's revolving door turns them back out on the street. STOP's mission is to lower the rate of convicted felons being released and returning to crime. I knew I couldn't do it all by myself, but I did all I could. I made speeches around town—at church and civic groups, victims' rights groups, radio stations. I sat on discussion panels with state representatives and held press conferences for the organization to raise awareness and lower the recidivism rate. I was interviewed often on television whenever there was a high profile crime. The people listening to my story would thank me. They looked at me and said, "If you can do it; I know I can do it." I sometimes received death threats on the phone for trying to keep people in prison. I told them to come on…I didn't care. STOP and my Stephen Ministry became the focus of my life.

I sat in on horrific trials in the area as support to others. Dorothy was a preacher's wife. She and her two daughters were abducted at gunpoint and taken to a secluded location. The killer murdered her daughters in front of Dorothy and sexually assaulted and shot her. I sat in on the trial which resulted in a conviction. Dorothy had a very forgiving spirit. She went to the prison to talk to the two men who had murdered her girls and asked why they did it. And she forgave them.

The burden of forgiveness is still heavy on me. I want to feel the way Dorothy felt, but I have a problem with unconditional forgiveness. I have to put my anger in a little package and lift it up to God. I hope He understands.

Sometimes parents came up to me after a trial and said they had a child in prison and were angry at what I was doing. They were against STOP and all we stood for. I really had to think about that. I had compassion for those families. We were just on opposite sides of the issue. Who knows how I would have felt if one of my children murdered someone? I was confident I was doing the right thing—victims' rights often seem to be lost in the effort to protect the rights of criminals. We agreed to disagree.

I received letters over the years from victims of crime who heard me speak. While I don't understand how I did anything by just telling my story, these people would tell me, "I heard you speak and it meant so much to me." I knew they were struggling as I was. If I said something to encourage them and they let me know it, then that was really healing for me as well. I have referenced portions of two of those letters below:

> *Dear Barbara,*
>
> *I have wanted to know you for years and to let you know what an impact your life has had on me. I first met you when you spoke to a class of Maitland's Citizen's Police Academy back in the mid-90s. I was then sponsored to attend the real police academy because of* **your** *presentation. I wanted to become a victim's advocate for the sheriff's department. I have enjoyed volunteering in different capacities since then. I am currently serving as caregiver to my mom, another friend from my church, as well as my husband and son. I wanted to let you know that your influence and inspiration have kept me sane when I feel overwhelmed by those I care for. I am grateful for your inspiration...*

And...

> *Dear Barbara,*
>
> *I talked to you at 3:00 p.m. and you were at a hearing at 4:45 p.m. Such short notice, but you were there and the support you showed*

*for perfect strangers meant so much to us. Not even people that are "supposed" friends were there, but you were.*

*I was moved by your motivation and am sorry, so sorry for your loss of your loved ones, but your strength is unlike anything I've ever seen. I only hope that one day I can be half the person you are.*

*On behalf of my daughter and myself...*

I have been blessed by the opportunity to help others through tough times.

\*\*\*

It took some time to come out of my isolation, but my eyes and my heart were finally open to new possibilities. Linda, the work friend who had come home with me after Charles's death, asked me to travel to Mexico with her. We were kindred spirits because she had lost a child in a car wreck just as I had. We flew to San Diego and rented a convertible to drive down the Baja peninsula to Ensenada for a ten-day stay. It was the first trip I had taken outside the U.S., other than the Caribbean cruises with Chuck, and it was a beautiful experience. I so appreciated the opportunity to get away.

A year or so after that, my neighbor, a world traveler and concert pianist, invited me to use her free companion airline ticket to fly anywhere in the world I wanted to go. Having no experience in the world of international travel, I left the destination up to her. She got back to me and asked, "How about Istanbul, Turkey?" That was the last place I expected, but she said the dollar was strong and we could get the most for our money. It turned out to be a wonderful stay in a five-star hotel. There was so much to learn about a different culture going through many of the architecturally magnificent mosques.

My world was getting broader—my sense of myself and the value of *me* increasing. It was exciting in a way. I was finally expecting good things to happen. I was getting a clearer sense of direction. I chose to live for the future and not in the past. A lot of people who lose a loved one will allow it to destroy their life. I hope my story will encourage others to, not get over their anger and grief, but to work through it. By letting others know how I did it, I want them to feel empowered to choose life. It is a healing joy for me to find that my story can help someone.

I was not the little girl playing tea party anymore. I wasn't focused on flowers, my hair-do or those other girly things. I no longer talked about how smart my children are or about the grandchildren I'll never have or about anything else in the past. I now wanted to be a part of the process of making my own and someone else's life better. I was focused on my ability to make choices in life and the accountability that goes with those choices. I talked to those who suffer life's tragedies and to victims of murder or rape. I stood alongside them as a friend who had been there. I was seeking answers, just as they were. Without yet knowing where I was going, I was willing to peer through just about any open door.

*Barbara with Poppy and Fritz*

FAILURE IS NOT THE OPPOSITE OF SUCCESS, RATHER, IT IS
THE ACT OF FALLING DOWN, FACING A CHALLENGE OR
ADVERSITY AND NOT GETTING BACK UP ON YOUR
FEET THAT DEFINES ONE AS A FAILURE."
NICK C. CICCHINO, MABC

"NOTHING CAN BRING YOU PEACE BUT YOURSELF."
RALPH WALDO EMERSON

## *Chapter Nine*

My Associate Degree was completed in 1995, after eight years of attending classes at night and fitting class work into my unique and uncommon life. In a meeting with the counselor at Rollins College, I was urged to walk across the stage to receive the degree. I hadn't planned to do that because it would, I thought, be upsetting for me to know how alone I was, with no one there to see me. This was a difficult decision. I asked for help from my usual source, "Okay, God, let's go. You gotta get me across that stage somehow." It was an emotional experience, but I was glad I did it.

Working toward my Bachelor's Degree in Organizational Communication, I had the chance to take a few classes that were of real value to my emotional well-being. One of the best was called *Hanging Loose in an Uptight World*. This class taught relaxation techniques and we learned how to project ourselves into another realm of reality to calm our heart rate and stress level. Mentally projecting oneself onto a relaxing beach scene, feeling the heat of the sun, feeling the wind, hearing the seagulls, smelling the salty air. I used this technique to keep calm while sitting through all the courtroom drama and it helped a lot. Lying in bed at night, I would use the technique of self-relaxation by taking a deep breath and mentally saying, *legs relax, heart relax, shoulders relax, arms, jaw, face, brain—each in its turn, relax.* Then I prayed before drifting off to sleep.

My nighttime meditations often ended like this: *My arms are warm, tingly and heavy. They are weighted and feel like Jello. My heart is calm and relaxed. My breath is slow and deep. I am relaxed. I hear the sound and surf and feel the sun. I am one with God who is at my side. All my stress is gone. I am in tune with the universe. Still…quiet…calm…relaxed. My problems I give over to God and lift them to the sky as I gain strength from the sun. The gulls fly so freely and rhythm of the surf affords healing within my being. I am content with myself. I am ready to take my life back with a renewed strength and calmness. I thank God for holding my cares as I leave my footprints in the sand to gain new insight to my future.*

I also used a mental blackboard, picturing myself writing my stresses on the board with chalk, then imagining picking up the eraser to wipe the board clean and replacing those stressful thoughts with the positive things I was doing in my life. I believe these relaxation and calming techniques are invaluable to anyone going through any sort of major or minor stress.

Another class that held great value for me was *Non-Fiction Creative Writing.* The assignment that clicked my emotional switch in a good way was to write to a loved one, living or deceased, to tell the person how you felt, and then to write a reply from that person. This was my chance to say some of the things I had longed to say to her and I wrote the following letter to my mother:

*Dear Mom,*

*I'm still quite mad at you for dying and leaving me alone at age fourteen. But still my heart aches for you to hold me all snuggled on your lap.*

*Thank you so much for all the things you taught me. I never realized just how smart you were way back then in the 1950s.*

*You have two beautiful grandchildren, Mom. Their names are Chuck and Jeff, but I guess you know them by now. What is it like in heaven? Are you with your grandchildren now?*

*Come to see me in my dreams often, Mom. By the way, I love you!*

The reply I wrote is as follows:

*Dear Barbara,*

*Honey, please don't be upset. I didn't want to leave you. Actually, I've been beside you every day for all your life. I'm so proud of you.*

*As for heaven, it is home now and, yes, every day someone appears that I recognize. Some come by choice; others not by choice.*

*Barbara, Chuck is playing golf. He just teed up on the 14th. Jeff and Charles are sitting in the boat hoping to catch 'the big one.' We are all okay, honey, and we take each step that you take every day. We are right beside you all the way.*

*Love and kisses—See you in your dreams...*

A simple process, yet it was a vibrant, restorative experience.

To celebrate my earning the BA Degree in Organizational Communication in 1998, Charles' sister, Syble, her husband, Rex, and their daughter, Karen with her husband, came down from Greenville, South Carolina for the graduation. It was so comforting to have their support. We marked the occasion with a celebratory dinner in my honor at Antonio's Restaurant in Maitland, along with Charles' brother-in-law, his wife, their two daughters and their husbands. I felt I was climbing a ladder. I didn't know where the ladder was leading me, but I knew I was going up instead of down.

My job with Sprint had been phased out when the company moved the Accounting Department to Kansas City. I was fortunate to get a secretarial position at Rollins College which included the benefit of free tuition. That was the only way I could have finished school. Textbooks were my only expense.

I wanted to continue working toward my Master's Degree. My job at Rollins had great benefits, but the paycheck was small. After earning my undergraduate degree, I left that position to go to work for Troy State (now Troy University). My position was that of Coordinator. I went to different sheriff's departments and military bases to set up classes for members of those entities to work toward a college degree while still serving. If there was enough interest at the sheriff's department or the military base to warrant setting up a class, I would act as liaison between the teachers and students. Among the degrees offered were Criminal Justice, Counseling and Psychology.

A benefit of working for Troy State was, again, free tuition, along with better pay than I had been receiving at Rollins. After achieving my Master's Degree at Troy, it was time for me to leave that job. The branch manager at Keller Graduate School approached me and asked if I would like to work for them as Assistant Director of Admissions. It was a good job with good pay and I accepted.

While I had thought about going for my doctorate, I was education-weary and needed to concentrate on my financial future with the hope of earning that PhD later.

\*\*\*

In life, there is more to an education than attending classes, and my next jobs were different types of learning experiences. I went to work for an American Express Financial Planner. Now that I had my education, I knew I needed a financial plan for the rest of my life—and what better way to learn about it than to work in the field? I learned a lot about the financial world and a few years later, I left that occupation for another new and different line of work.

My car was getting old. I began looking in the paper for jobs and spotted an ad for a car salesperson. I had been in sales for years and needed to know the ropes about buying a car, so I thought, why not sell them? I walked into the dealership, said I wanted to interview for a job, and they hired me. I sold Chevys in Winter Park at Holler Chevrolet, a company with several dealerships in the area. I worked on the floor selling cars for close to a year. They asked me to transfer to the corporate headquarters and manage the internet sales for the Chevrolet division, which I did for about another year. While I made considerable money on the sales floor, the company downgraded the internet sales division and my income went down along with it.

*Coordinator/Cohort of off campus studies*

"LET GO OF WHAT WAS. SURRENDER TO WHAT IS. HAVE
FAITH IN WHAT WILL BE."
SONIA RICOTTI

# *Chapter Ten*

L ife had settled into a routine. I was free-floating through this stage, working for Holler Motor Company, continuing my work with the Stephen Ministry through my church and doing public speaking to promote the mission of STOP and MADD (Mothers Against Drunk Driving). I had a few women friends who knew my story, but, for the most part, making friends and getting close to someone was a challenge. I am everybody's worst nightmare. I know I am. Nobody wants to think about the life I've led. People are afraid to bring up the subject of children knowing what happened to mine. I guess they worry about what they would do if I started to cry or something. It's frustrating really. They don't want to talk about their kids because they don't want to hurt me, and I don't want to talk about my kids because I don't want to make them uncomfortable. It is a negative vibe on a relationship. I discovered the answer to the dilemma is to just be myself. We've all had some tragedy in our lives—losing a parent, spouse, child...or maybe a tragic fire that consumed your home and all your worldly possessions or fighting an illness—every one of us has been through life's wringer at some point.

For the first year or two, it's probably best not to approach a person's tragedies unless they bring it up first. If they're having a good day, you want them to have that good day. But after some time passes, you can't act like someone's loved ones never existed. As humans, we want and need to reflect on those memories. It is only natural, when we meet someone new, to ask if they have children or grandchildren. If I tell a new acquaintance my children are in heaven, it puts a cloud over the conversation. I want them to talk about their families, but I want to talk about mine too. The uncomfortable shift in the tone of the conversation becomes apparent. The situation becomes awkward and that's really not right. I love to talk about how my boys played baseball and football, how they were on the swim team and excelled in their private Christian school. My boys had a normal life, and they are alive in my happiest memories.

Evolution and adaptation coupled with tragedy and grief yield psychological stresses that can result in deadly consequences. My memories and dreams were shattered along with my family and that brought me to my knees in search of peace and answers as to *WHY ME GOD?* I use the stress management techniques I gained in my college classes to guide me through sleepless nights and the fear of the unknown. I cannot erase my stressful past, but I can strive for a more internal locus of control that allows me peace.

The people I could relate to best were those I helped in my volunteer work. Though I didn't babble on about my experiences, just having somebody with my background to listen to them and truly understand the depth of their suffering was their life preserver in turbulent waters. I don't have any more answers than anyone else. I'm just there to listen and there is tremendous power in listening. My work brought me fulfillment and affirmation. I was learning who I am and what makes me happy. My self-confidence was back.

***

The year was 2007. I had no intention of searching for a new husband and had a private joke with God as I prayed, "God, if you send me a husband, he's going to have to come knocking on my door, because I am *not* getting out there and looking."

I became interested in computers and the internet created an opportunity for me to connect with friends back in Birmingham. Curious about what had become of my classmates from Phillips High School, I joined an online group called *reunion.com* and filled out a profile.

I had a response from a fellow named Ed Colvin saying, "Do you remember me?" I responded in the affirmative as I remembered both he and his wife Becky who was in a class or two ahead of us. Ed shared that he and Becky had been married for forty-six years when she passed away two years prior. I had run into him and his wife at several high school reunions over the years, and I'm sure we all said 'hello' to one another. I had written about my family situation and story in my personal bio for the reunion memory book, so he knew a bit about my life. Ed and I began a friendly email chat back and forth for several weeks.

One day he sent me a message, "I'm coming through Milton, driving through the Florida panhandle with my daughter and grandson. Can I stop by and buy you a cup of coffee?" The coffee part was fine with me, except I had given a different hometown in my profile. I was extra-cautious about sharing personal information on the internet, so I had declined to put my true location online for all to see. I answered him, "Well, I really don't live in Milton, I live in Maitland, just north of Orlando." Another week or so passed and he contacted me to say he had a son living in Stuart, Florida down on the east coast and would be visiting him right after Christmas. Could he come through Orlando to buy me that cup of coffee?

Ed dealt with his grief at losing his wife in a unique way. He wrote his thoughts in little notes to his Becky expressing his feelings and to maintain their special connection. In November of 2007, he wrote the following:

> *"I did a crazy thing last night. I paid for a subscription to Reunion.com so I could email Barbara Benton. You remember her from Phillips High. She lives in Milton, Florida. For some reason I feel drawn to make contact with her. She looks great and is probably too classy for me but, what the hell, if I don't try it may be like 'Some Enchanted Evening' and I will spend all my days alone."*

Just five days later, he wrote:

> *"I have been thinking about Barbara Benton the past few days and, for some reason I get excited getting her messages and look forward to them. I wish she were in Milton instead of Orlando. I am like a school boy. Pretty silly of me to feel this way."*

And so he came to see me in January of 2008 on his way to visit his son. I picked Ed up at his Winter Park hotel about eight o'clock the morning after his arrival. We talked and had breakfast. We walked up and down Park Avenue in Winter Park. We toured the Morse Museum and went to the museum at Rollins College. While at the museum, we passed by an extraordinary set of stained glass doors with a sign above that said "Knock and it shall be opened for you." I was captivated by that sentiment, thinking it prophetic and…yes…I walked over and knocked on that door. There was no instant message from heaven, but a guard immediately came over and reprimanded me, "Ma'am, please don't knock on the door!" The day was passing quickly and my dogs needed walking, so Ed and I went to my condo to take care of the dog walking. Then we went for lunch together.

We had only planned to touch base briefly, but we were comfortable together—like a pipe and slippers. We were not trying to impress each other. We talked of old friends and high school days and it felt right. We took in a movie. Did the mile walk around Lake Eola several times. Had dinner. Had a late cup of coffee. Around nine or ten o'clock I took him back to his hotel. The next morning he left to see his son.

One of my volunteer activities was chairing the volunteers for the Orlando Festival of Orchestras. We brought in orchestras from all over the world to perform at the Bob Carr Theater in Orlando. There were major orchestras coming in about four times a year. I asked Ed to join me for one of the concerts on his way back to Birmingham. He said he would like that and that next week I picked him up at his hotel and we went to the concert. Eva, a friend of mine, was with us for the concert. Ed thought I had invited a chaperone, but after dropping Eva at her home, we went out for pie and coffee.

One week later, I received this message by email:

*"Barbara, my love...I can hardly believe it was just a week ago that we sat and talked in the coffee shop after the concert. I went to Orlando without a hope for the future and now everything in my world has changed so much for the better now that you are part of it. I have a future since I have met you again.*

*"Today when I went to church it was so different with my thoughts and spirit. I kept saying, 'Thank you, God.' The weather was cloudy, but at the end of the service, as we were standing to sing the last song, the sun came through the stained glass window and it seemed to shine*

*on me. I don't know if I believe in signs, but somehow it made me think that it was sort of a blessing and that we will have something special.*

*"Can't wait until you're in my arms again. I will be calling you.*

*"I love you, Barbara Rowe…. Ed"*

That note stopped me in my tracks, and I remember breathing deeply and thinking, "Be still my heart." I was wary of letting myself be vulnerable again. Until that moment, I was not even thinking along the lines of a future with this man; I was having a nice, enjoyable time with an old friend. We started sending each other songs by email. He made another trip to Orlando to visit.

Many times through my life I had asked God, "Where's the good stuff?" Well, here was my answer. Ed is the good stuff. I felt that God hand-picked him just for me. He literally did come knocking on my door.

I wanted to give our relationship time to grow, but I was afraid of it too. We began creating a story and emailing segments back and forth. I would write two or three paragraphs and pass it off to him to write two or three paragraphs.

I couldn't believe it. Here Ed was, larger than life at six feet tall. I was at a stage in my life where I thought I would be enjoying grandchildren. This was an opportunity to have some step-grandchildren. It was frightening in an exhilarating way. I tried to warn Ed that even my artificial plants wilt and die. He was not discouraged.

The marriage proposal came by email…from across the room. Ed thought since the relationship had started by email, it would be appropriate and fun to propose that way, even though he was in the same room with me.

I lived in Orlando. Ed lived in Birmingham. He wanted his two sons and one daughter to know me and accept me, so he took me to Birmingham to meet his family. The first meeting was uncomfortable for me. After all, he'd been married to Becky for forty-six years. She'll always be their mother and grandmother and I would never try to fill that role. Even though that meeting seemed awkward, I hope by now they've truly accepted me.

I responded positively to his declaration of love and the marriage proposal; I wasn't going to let him get away. We knew we weren't getting any younger and didn't want to waste a lot of time. Four months after that first email, we married secretly. The wedding took place at the courthouse on March 26, 2008, while I was on my lunch hour. We kept it a secret so we could plan a second wedding in Birmingham with Ed's family involved.

Ed moved in with me in Orlando with his large Malamute and his love seat recliner. In my den I only had one chair and, as Ed put it, "it wasn't big enough for both of us."

In Birmingham, Ed had been living in a house he and his daughter Jennifer had purchased. Jennifer was divorced, and Ed wanted her to get out of the apartment she was living in and have a home to raise her son, Dylan. One day, after what seemed like a normal phone conversation, Jennifer casually asked him, "By the way, are you and Barbara married?" Ed was caught off-guard and said, "Why do you ask?"

She said, "Well, there was a letter in the mail addressed to Barbara Colvin from the medical insurance company." So much for keeping the marriage a secret—we'd been caught! Of course, we then had to tell everyone we were married, and we never did have that second ceremony in Birmingham.

We stay in touch with Ed's family and go to Birmingham or to his son's house near Huntsville a few times a year at Easter, Christmas and Thanksgiving. Not living closer, there hasn't been a lot of opportunity for me to build a solid relationship with Ed's children, but I think they have accepted me as his wife. In fact, Jennifer once said to me, "Thank you for saving my dad's life." His children all knew Ed was devastated when their mother died. It seems I was the only one he thought he might be able to build another life with. For that, I am very grateful too.

Now that the secret was out about our wedding, we thought about moving closer to his family in Birmingham. That was fine with me. Florida had not been good for me, and I never wanted to be there in the first place. It was in Florida that I had lost my whole family. I did have a desire to be where *southern* people are—where ladies are ladies and people say hello when you pass them on the street. Florida has a different, more hurried, culture.

Together we looked at Newman, Georgia as a retirement destination. Oddly, just as Charles and I had run off to Georgia to get married so many years before, so had Ed and his Becky. It seemed to be the place for young lovers to wed—perhaps they have more lenient marriage requirements. Now some of those same folks are moving there to retire.

In our search for our new home, Ed and I visited Fairhope, Alabama, and I fell in love with the place. For many years, he and his family had vacationed at the beach in Gulf Shores, and he and Becky had come to Fairhope often. It felt comfortable to him.

Winter Park, Florida is an artsy little college town with plays and concerts and charm. We were looking for something similar. Fairhope filled our expectations with its magical bayfront park, quaint shops and restaurants and busy cultural life. We worked with a realtor, telling her we wanted a formal dining room, a fireplace, and a fenced-in yard for our "blended" family of three dogs. The home we found has none of these things, but we can walk out on our deck that sits right down on a tranquil little lake. I knew it would be a peaceful, healing place. "This is it," we told the realtor. I walk outside on the deck in the morning and hear the ducks out there laughing. In the afternoon the seagulls fly over raucously conversing with one another. No formal dining room, no fireplace and no fenced-in yard, but it is the right house for us.

I thank God for Ed every day, and I think he would say the same. Life here is good. We go to orchestra concerts on the bayside bluff, see performances at the community theater, stay active in our church, and attend events at the busy local arts center. Many evenings, we go down to the bay with a glass of wine and watch the fiery sunset. Life is never perfect, but this is close.

I am a lover of mountains; Ed prefers the beach. And so, we do a little of both. Every year we rent a hillside home that overlooks several mountain ranges in North Carolina. We sit in the hot tub with our glasses of wine and watch the sun dip down behind the mountains. When I'm in those mountains I feel closer to heaven, and it heals my heart. We live close enough to the Gulf of Mexico to take day trips to the white sand beach and listen to the pounding surf of the Gulf.

I've lived enough of life to know that you can never know what comes next, but for now, just for now, I am reveling in my version of the "good stuff." And I know I am strong enough to handle whatever my future might bring—just like the massive Live Oak trees that surround me here and weather storms, wind and drought along with the days of sunshine and refreshing, gentle rain. I am content.

## The Oak Tree

A mighty wind blew night and day.
It stole the Oak Tree's leaves away.
Then snapped its boughs and pulled its bark
Until the Oak was tired and stark.

But still the Oak Tree held its ground
While other trees fell all around.
The weary wind gave up and spoke,
"How can you still be standing, Oak?"

The Oak Tree said, I know that you
Can break each branch of mine in two,
Carry every leaf away,
Shake my limbs and make me sway.

But I have roots stretched in the earth,
Growing stronger since my birth.
You'll never touch them, for you see
They are the deepest part of me.

Until today, I wasn't sure
Of just how much I could endure.
But now I've found with thanks to you,
I'm stronger than I ever knew.

*By Johnny Ray Ryder, Jr.*

*Ed, Rocky, Barbara, Jack and Russell*

# ACKNOWLEDGEMENTS

Thank you to my loving husband, Joseph Edward Colvin, for patience and inspiration. And thank you all God's angels who walked beside me during the good, tragic, and happy moments in my life. If your name is among these, I am deeply indebted to you: Lou and Alice Robinson, Police Chief Guy Calhoun, Dr. Debbie Douglas, Rex and Syble McBryde, Fonda McGowan, Linda Boyle, and Jack Daily.

Finally my gratitude to the incredible people who helped me put my story on paper: Rosanne Gulisano, Lynn White, Jack Daily, Dr. Bob Zeanah, Dr. Ann Pearson, and Reverend Laura Parker. If I have missed someone, I truly apologize and thank you.

Special heartfelt gratitude to Jack Daily who designed the cover, gave feedback, and encouraged me to write this book.

Dr. Ann Pearson, Director of Caring Ministries, Fairhope United Methodist Church said "Barbara is a tower of resilience in circumstances that have impacted and altered her life forever. Her faith enables her to bring hope, care and understanding to others."

# ABOUT THE AUTHOR

Having survived the death of her sixteen year old son to vehicular homicide in 1980, the death of her husband of thirty-two years to violent crime in 1992, and the death of her oldest son to AIDS in 1993, Barbara shares her story in hopes of helping others survive tragic life events.

Barbara earned a BA in Organizational Communication in 1998 from Rollins College in Winter Park, Florida and an MS in Counseling and Psychology in 2000 from Troy University in Winter Park, Florida. Currently, Barbara is active at Fairhope United Methodist Church in Fairhope, Alabama, and volunteers as a Stephen Minister.

Previously Barbara's story was featured in *Profiles in Character* by Jeb Bush and Brian Yablonski; *Orlando Magazine*, "*Meet Central Florida's 25 Most Intriguing Personalities*"; and numerous local newspaper articles. In 1996, the Victim Services Coalition of Orange and Osceola counties gave her its award for "outstanding commitment to victims of crime." Barbara served as Vice Chair of the State Board of Directors and President of the Central Florida Chapter of STOP. (Stop Turning Out Prisoners), a statewide organization dedicated to reversing the current standard of early release for felons convicted of violent crime. She has spoken to community service groups and law enforcement organizations throughout the state of Florida and has been the subject of articles and interviews by the *Orlando Sentinel,* and many radio and television stations.

"Being proactive was a great healing vehicle during the grief process for me."

Barbara currently resides in Fairhope, Alabama, with her husband Ed Colvin and their blended canine family of three dogs. She is available as a speaker to share her story. Contact Barbara at myjourneytoo@yahoo.com.

Made in the USA
Charleston, SC
22 February 2015